UNDERSTANDING
RELATIONSHIPS
AND
HOW TO IMPROVE THEM

Ida Greene, PhD

Understanding Relationships and How to Improve Them

Copyright © January 2, 2015, P. S. I. Publishers, 2910 Baily Ave. San Diego, CA 92105

ISBN 978-1-881165-25-5

ATTENTION COLLEGES AND UNIVERSITIES, CORPORATIONS, and PROFESSIONAL ORGANIZATIONS:

Quantity discounts are available on bulk purchases of this book for educational training purposes, fund raising, or gift giving.

For Information Contact: P. S. I. Publishers, 2910 Baily Avenue, San Diego, CA 92105, (619) 262-9951 www.journeytoselflove.com.

E-mail: ida@thejourneytoselflove.com

CONTENTS

Introduction 5

Chapter 1: Facing the Inner Demon of Lost Love 7

Chapter 2: What is Love and How Do You Get It or Find It?..21

Chapter 3: The Pillars of a Good Relationship 41

Chapter 4: How Your Family Communication Patterns Affect Your Relationship 67

Chapter 5: Follow Your Passion to Find Love 81

Chapter 6: How to Find the Love You Want 89

Introduction

This book is designed to help you with those nagging relationship concerns you have been afraid to ask or approach. It will answer some of your most daunting questions about relationships and how to make them work. Effective relationships are an art form and is always in a fluid, engaging and dynamic state of evolution. It is a delicate dance between getting to know a person and finding a good and comfortable fit for both you and them.

In a new relationship you do not want to move in too quickly, and you do not want to seem detached or dis-engaged. It is best to start any new relationship with a heart- warming connectional conversation, give the person a genuine acknowledgement, then develop curiosity to get to know more about them. Find out, what is their greatest concern and how you can serve them.

Everyone wants to know how much you care about them and their pressing concerns. We need to always answer the question, what is in the conversation or relationship for the other person. When you show you have the other person's best interest in the fore front of your mind, they will feel your caring, your compassion and love for them. This will increase their likeness of you and increase your likeability factor with them.

We never want to been seen by others as someone who is manipulative, cunning or as someone who is only interested in themselves and what you can get form the other person. I describe these people as human sharks or human vultures. Who will never receive the Dale Carnegie award for "How to Win Friends and Influence People". Everyone is an unknown entity, so expect to experience some frustration with some of your relationships. When we move from frustration to apathy we no longer care. So try to have compassion for the people who enter your life. None of us are perfect, we are all a work of art in progress, in the eyes of God.

In a relationship we can only control and change ourselves, and we can positively influence others. Trying to control another person is an unwinnable game. Human beings cannot be controlled but can be influenced positively; if we play the relationship game of life in a way, where we use our communication skills, ideas, love and compassionate energy to create a positive outcome between us and the people with whom we relate.

People are the elixir of life. They are the key ingredient you will need, to create your relationships which may be a: friendship, family relationship, platonic relationship, romantic relationship, love relationship, or a relationship to start and grow your business.

This book will give you the foundation and the people skills you need to develop and master to be a success in all relationships. I love meeting new people and establishing new authentic relationships, what about you?

Chapter 1

Facing the Inner Demon
of Lost Love

If you have been single for a while and you are now ready to have a new love relationship, you can expect to have anxiety from your past relationships show up which can cloud how you enter into or approach a new relationship. You also may feel that finding that special someone will make everything in your life "better". If you spend your time and energy looking for your "better half" you will have feelings of inadequacy and incompletion. The odds are that you are doing things that are counterproductive to inviting love into your life. When you start to look for love you will need to clear away the emotional and physical clutter of your life to make room for love.

Another thing you will want to do is to let the lover or lost lover that "got away" go away. Do you feel that if timing or circumstances had been just a bit different your relationship would have worked? The strange thing about the past is that sometimes it can appear better from a distance. Maybe you have not taken the time to work through the hurt feelings and reasons why your lost love did not work. In order to move into a new relationship you need to let go of the things that did not work and focus your energy on what you are trying to achieve now. You may want to let go of the perfect Boyfriend/ girlfriend from your past. Take notice of what you liked about your past lover and remember it as a happy memory rather than as an impediment that will keep you in the past or keep you depressed and prevent you from moving forward. It paints a mental picture from your inner belief of who you think you can be, or what you believe you can have in your life.

Your self-esteem is a blueprint of who you are and how you have been treated, respected, appreciated, and identified by those around you. Your self-esteem is endless; it is the essence of who you are, not what anyone may see you as. It is fragile. It can be affected by many factors and needs continual maintenance. It reflects how you view yourself; how you honor, respect, and value yourself. It paints a mental picture or inner belief of who you think you can be in a relationship or what you believe you can do in your life.

Your self-esteem is the vehicle you use to move through life to achieve your goals. It is the package you create to get the things you want or to reach the goals you have set for yourself. Each person has a separate agenda, determined by what he or she is called to do in this lifetime. If your self-esteem is wholesome, and you feel good about yourself, you can accomplish great things. If your self-esteem is damaged, or less than what it could be, your ability to accomplish or achieve will be hampered by a negative self-concept. That negative picture will create a self-image that tells you that you are less than others, not good enough, that you cannot or will not be successful in your love life. We are each marching to a different drummer. Each person is unique and different. We need to see ourselves as kind, understanding, and powerful. Remember who you are is Spirit's gift to you, and what you make of yourself is your gift to Spirit.

We are all born to develop, create, change, and die. Nothing is static. Everything is in motion, a continuous energy transformation. We are born anew each hour. This is why it does us no good to hold on to the experiences of the past. If you rely only on your human ego, which is cold calculating, judgmental, and without feeling or compassion, you will experience needless pain and suffering.

A negative self-image reminds us continually that we cannot measure up to the standards of society. It matters not whether this is fact or fiction; if this belief held by an individual, it will hamper the contribution they make in life because they will be looking through a distorted mirror that will reflect a distorted image and message back to them that says, "I am different from others, I am not okay." Depending on our self-concept, self-belief, self-image, and self-respect, we will rise to great heights or fall to the depths of great despair. So let go of the notion that there is a perfect relationship or a perfect person you need to meet for you to be happy or find happiness in life.

There is no such thing as a perfect person or perfect relationship; besides perfect is a boring idea of what a relationship is or can be. I think it is helpful to write down the list of traits you want in a partner as well as deal breakers, but use this information a guideline to lessen your anxiety to start you on your journey to love and self-fulfillment. When you make your list of traits for what you want in a new lover and your deal breakers for the new lover, try to make sure that your list of qualities and traits addresses not just the surface traits like green eyes, brown hair, and chiseled features, but that it includes deeper qualities that address who they are as a person and who how they interact with others as couple or in a couple relationship. For example:

- Are they a morning person?

- Do they like to watch funny movies?

- What do they consider to be a romantic date?

- How do they like to spend a lazy afternoon?

- Do they like to share their emotions?

- Do they know how to have arguments in a healthy way?

Again, these lists are more for you to help tune your brain and heart towards being aware of the people who are a good fit for you. It is not to build a fortress of perfection that no one will ever be able to reach. Remember, all people have flaws, relationships are not perfect, and if you can allow for this ebb and flow of relationships to occur, it will make it much easier for you find a potential lover who is a good match for you. Be open to what the universe has to offer. You may find that the best surprises and connections arrive in a different package than what you expected.

Anyone can create a new image and increase our self esteem by changing their thoughts about their self-worth, taking more risks in life, changing their thoughts and feelings on love, accepting that they are worthy and deserving of love, showing gratitude for the small ways love shows up in their life, avoiding feeling sorry for themselves when love does not show up in the way they would like, and taking small action steps to create a loving relationship. If you sit waiting for love to find you, you may be waiting for a long time. You will have to set yourself and your heart on fire with the passion of love so someone can see your flame. You do not need to grovel and allow someone to treat you without respect to be loved. Love is not abuse and abuse and disrespect are not love. These are some of the issues you need to look at so your self-esteem and self-worth are healthy and intact:

1. Ask for what you want without creating drama around your asking.

2. Take a risk, step out of your comfort zone, and relate in a genuine way, not as a victim wanting sympathy or pity.

3. Own what you are doing wrong. Are you playing the role of a victim? If so, is it because you do not feel you deserve better, or did you learn from your mom how to play a victim role? Is this is your role or purpose in life? Are unwilling to learn and grow for fear you will lose the people around you? Are you playing the role of a victim so others can love you, to have a family, to keep a family, to keep a husband, a child, or a lover?

4. Do not equate love with abuse and suffering.

5. Eliminate the feeling that love is long suffering

6. Be grateful for what you have.

7. Give up feeling no one will love you unless you let them treat you like the dirt on the ground they walk on.

8. Stop wanting others to feel sorry for how they treat you and when they don't, stop thinking you are getting what you feel you deserve and want.

9. Others will treat you the way you allow them to treat you.

10. When you make yourself a rug or carpet, people will walk all over you. Do not do it.

11. Do you love yourself? If not, why not?

12. Do you feel you deserve to be treated in a loving way?

13. Do you feel you deserve respect?

14. Where did you learn or who showed you how to be a door mat, to be treated like a slave, or like a "nobody"?

15. Do you have courage and do you take responsibility for the role you play in the way your relationships are unfolding?

16. Don't let others be responsible for your self-esteem, to be your jury, or to decide what happens in your life.

17. Everyone is responsible for creating their own joy, their love, their self-respect, their self-worth, their health, and the life they want to live.

18. You can be authentic and real, or you can be a victim.

19. You can stand up for yourself, or you can let others treat you as they want to treat you.

20. You can live like a peasant or a Queen/King, but you can't be both.

21. You can believe in yourself and work to improve yourself and your life. You can live with love, self-worth, and self-esteem.

22. Do you have the courage to love yourself even if you are the only one except Spirit who loves you?

We All Need the Following to Be Whole and Complete:

Security: Self-acceptance, a sense of belonging to someone or something.

Identity: Self-description to given you by your family of origin.

Support: Mental, physical, and emotional.

Desire: Dreams, visions, or goals.

Self-Esteem: Internal belief about yourself and the way you experience life. The five parts of self-esteem are self-concept, self-image, self-worth, self-respect, and self-confidence.

A. Self-Concept = Personal and Spiritual Identity

B. Self-Image = Inner picture of how you see yourself, reflects outside you

C. Self-Respect = Positive self-regard

D. Self-Worth = Importance to family, society, life (Spirit)

E. Self-Confidence = Self-assurance, comfort, inner peace

Spirituality: Your anchor, your purpose for living to contribute, and make a difference.

Aesthetic Appreciation: Non-human, a sense of awe and majesty. We develop a sense of Security by having our birth and existence validated by someone other than ourselves. Someone, who by their words, actions, and deeds says, "I am glad you were born." If you get this message from a core family member, it adds to your self-worth and self-acceptance, and helps to create a feeling of belonging and importance.

A positive Self-Concept enables us to accept ourselves, in spite of our shortcomings or perceived deficiencies. If we acknowledge ourselves as a work of fine art, a masterpiece constantly evolving, we accept ourselves as we are with the capacity to improve and to become better. Our self-concept is not one, but two-dimensional. Our self-concept is greatly influenced by our thoughts, feelings, and actions. As one of Spirit's creations, we are each in the possession of a Personal Self-Concept Identity and a Spiritual Self-Concept Identity; a Self-Image (inner self-picture) is formed based on the concept we have of ourselves.

Your Identity, used interchangeably with the term Self-Concept, is the core aspect of you. Because of it, there are no two people alike. Spirit created everyone different and unique.

Therefore, you are special, one of a kind. Spirit has built within each person a spiritual yardstick to which we should all strive to measure up to. Each lesson is as equally challenging and hard for each person. It is decided before we come to earth the best conditions (parents, race, sex, e.g.) to help us grow and blossom spiritually. The human experience is a refining process necessary for our soul to evolve and develop.

Spirit allows us to decide the particulars of how we want to live our life and what we want to do or accomplish. Some of us decide to come to earth to give joy to our parents for a day, a year, 7 years, or 70 years. Whatever we do with our life, it must be a masterpiece for all to behold. And since no one knows when the final hour will be, it is best that we make each day count. You must do your best daily to be the best person you can be. Sometimes you do not get a second chance to clear up a destructive or unproductive life. It is easy to look at another person and wish you were more like them. Yet, you do not know the pain they endure behind the smile. Remember, you chose this lifetime. You said yes to the Universe and to your life circumstances. The Divine Spirit never promised any of us that we would live a life free of hardship or challenge.

Life is an unpainted canvas. You can create as many scenes as you like. Life is a journey, not a destination. When you stop growing you slowly die, so pause if you must. Take time to enjoy the scenery and the stage production you created. When you die and leave the planet, will your life and living be a masterpiece, or will you give back the heap of ashes from which you came? Who you are is beautiful and magnificent. You are one of a kind, a rare gem.

Your Self-Concept is the basic foundation of who you are. To be fully the person the Divine intended you to be, it will require that you develop both your Personal and Spiritual Self-Concept.

Most of us spend little time developing our Spiritual Self-Concept. It is just as important as your Personal Self-Concept. Both aspects of your nature need to be cultivated and built up. Our other basic human needs are support, desire, and self-esteem.

Support – Our Mental, Physical, Emotional Body - We achieve maturity and grow spiritually by working on our mental, physical, and emotional bodies. We have an inner drive to achieve, excel, and be a better person to gain mastery over our lower nature to become the Christ within. We have been given a physical body to work through our imperfections, our negative emotions, and our thoughts of self-doubt. Your goal is to seek ways to improve these three aspects of yourself. This provides the self-discipline you need to complete your primary goal of soul perfection.

Desire – A Dream or a Goal - Believe in yourself, and know you are valuable to life. Like yourself enough to have goals. Be willing to take risks, or plan how you will live your life. The ability to dream or envision a goal is Spirit's divine plan to inspire us to reach and stretch beyond our human limitations. Most big goals, and some little goals, require us to partner with Spirit for their completion and success. Dreams are the longings placed inside of us to help maintain our connection to "It." These are the attributes of a spiritually and whole person:

Love/ Unconditional, Acceptance, Empathy, Peace, Harmony, Joy, Kindness, Compassion, Tranquility, Gentleness, Consolation, Understanding, Excellence, and Creativity.

Self-Esteem – Our self-concept has many parts; our self-esteem is composed of many selves. Your self-esteem is determined by your cultural upbringing, your morals, and the values of your individual and cultural identities. Your self-esteem tells others how you think and feel about yourself and your relationships with others.

Webster's dictionary defines it as "A confidence and satisfaction in oneself." The California State Task Force on Self-Esteem defines it as "Appreciating my own worth, and importance, and having the character to be accountable for myself and to act responsibly towards others."

The way you act is a measure of your self-esteem. You can find more detailed information on this topic in my book *Self-Esteem the Essence of You* at www.idagreene.com

What is Smallness?

Smallness is a state of contraction. The Strength and Source of your Power is on the outside. When you are consumed and controlled by the daily activities that happen to you, you expect the worst outcome because you usually have more bad things than good things happen to you. Your relationships are in disarray, negative, unfulfilling, empty, unrewarding, unloving, petty, vengeful, controlling, conflicting, and constricting.

When your gains in life outweigh your pains, you are on the road to know and experience your Greater Self. Focus your energy by living your vision. Start living now as if everything you desire in life is already in your life, including the right person. Get into the feeling nature of being the best you that you can be. Find out what matters to you and do something about it. When you are attractive, you do not have to wait; you create and draw to you what you desire. Just make sure that when the right person shows up, you have something to share with him or her. These are just some of the things to consider that will help you decide if you have effectively moved through your lost love or if it is still affecting your self-esteem.

What is Greatness?

Greatness is a mindset of excellence. You have an Inner Power that makes you calm, serene, and peaceful. You have feelings and an attitude of abundance and prosperity. You are able to manifest anything you desire in an instant. Everything you engage in is about Excellence. There is no discord or confusion in your life. What could keep you anchored is your "inner state of knowing" who you are and what you know for certain you can do.

Clear Up Old Baggage From Your Past

It takes courage to clear up the old baggage from our past. Sometimes it may feel easier to cram the feelings of the past down deep into the pit of our soul where it remains stuck as we trod along. Granted there are some things that you might want to set aside to deal with later, but at some point the emotional bill will come due. Eventually all those past hurts, resentments, and frustrations will find a way to burble up and generally at the most inopportune moments, and most definitely during the course of your romantic relationships.

Try this test: Consider how you feel when thinking about the potential of dating and meeting someone new. If your gut reaction is nausea, panic, stress, and basically to run the other way, it is likely have some baggage to sort through. The first step is to simply take inventory. Remember it's taken a long time to gather that baggage, so don't expect to find, clear, and move on from it in a day. It's not really possible to be baggage free, and some baggage can even be helpful—some protects us while we heal—but if you continuously operate on flawed criteria to look for love, it's going to make the search that much more challenging. Commit to tackling your baggage if only one small piece at a time.

Remember, it has taken you a long time; it may seem like a lifetime to collect your emotional baggage, hurts, and habits. Be kind to yourself and be patient in the process of clearing the clutter and energy so you can allow a loving relationship to take the place of what you've cleared away. In doing so, you are making room in your heart, mind, and life to clear the way for love to show up again.

How to Reclaim Your Power to Heal Your Inner Pain

We have all been wounded or hurt by someone. To be healed of your emotional wounds, you will need to let go of the stories in your head about who hurt you, when they hurt you, and how they hurt you. Become free from being a victim by choosing to be become detached from your recalled memory of past hurts and wounds. There will always be people who abuse or hurt us unintentionally by living their life as best they know how and being who they are.

Just because we are wounded does not mean we have to take on the role, play the role, or live out our life existence through the role of a victim, or become the "walking wounded". We often take things, people, and the situations that happen to us far too personally. Remember to not take everything that has happened to you in your life "personally".

Things happen and some things are just the way they are. There are billions of people on the planet like you, who are trying to figure why they are here and what they are supposed to do with this thing we have been given called LIFE. Your life is the Inner Power that has been given to you by Divine Spirit to show up and play a bigger game as a player of Greatness in the Game of Life.

Your Greatness is your Inner Power to Be to Do and to Have. It is time for you to reclaim your Power and live from Your Greatness. It is time to break through to your Greatness.

How to Break Through to Your Best Self
Write down everything that you're afraid of.

1.

2.

3.

4.

5.

6.

7.

How do you want to show up in the world? Do you have a belief about creating value for yourself?

What is it?

What can you do today to create value for yourself?

How can you create value for others through the way you live your life?

Our value in life is created by who we are as well as what we do. Others are watching us to see what use we make of our gifts, talents, and influence, because it determines our greatness.

Both women and men have low self-esteem issues. The uncertainty girls and women have about who they are, and if they are pretty, and if they are as pretty as their peers, and do they fit into the group, or will they find a guy to like or love them—and the comparison list goes on and on? It is no different with men; over 70% of men struggle to express their feelings, which trigger women to feel unsafe around them. Men often view sharing emotions as a sign of weakness.

Men get close through competition and taking action. Women get and feel close in a relationship through talking and sharing. Women want to be in love through connections with men, and to feel that they are important. Men fail at love because they don't treat it as a serious responsibility. Men tie this to their self-worth and feel they are not good as a man. Men lack emotional intelligence and situational awareness. Men don't feel safe to express their true feelings.

Men rarely reach out to support networks, therapists, or a life coach; instead they rely only on themselves. Both women and men press the self-sabotage button without even knowing it. Our ultimate goal is to live from our greatness.

Chapter 2

What is Love and How Do You Get It or Find It?

I say love is a "many splendid thing". It comes in many forms, languages, cultures, shapes, sizes, skin tones, beliefs, religions, relationships, emotions, feelings, work settings, family settings, sport settings, and in the mind and hearts of an individual.

Love is everywhere, yet most of us feel unloved, unwanted, not cared about, needed, or appreciated. If love is everywhere as I suspect it is; why do you think we are unable to see it, feel it, or detect its presence in our lives? Have you ever wondered about that? I have and sometimes I have to do a self-inventory to see if I am loved and to remind myself that I am loved. In addition, in many of our families, we do not verbally express our love or caring for each other, because we do not have the language or proper way to say what we want to share. In many cases it is assumed that our family members know we love them, and this could not be further from the truth. We are often not shown how to say or how to show that we care. It is much easier to share our negative thoughts than it is to share our positive thoughts and feelings.

The main way we show love is through our nonverbal and verbal communication. Although we are verbal communicators, we are nonverbal when it comes to love. We are not good verbal communicators when it comes to love. Partly because love is a heart-feeling connection that is not easily understood, so most of us do not know how to express love or show love. We are not taught or trained on how to show our love or our caring, therefore we do not know how to do it, and we often do not recognize love when it shows up in our lives. This is because love has to do with the quality and value of our communication and we are deficient when it comes to communicating what we value, who we value, in what way we value it or them. As a child I felt my mom did not love me; however, as an adult I realized that my mom showed her love for me by focusing on my being more ladylike, because I was constantly climbing, sitting with my legs open, and exposing my underwear. She also showed her love for me by preparing my favorite food for me. My mom gave us all love through food. It can be difficult to explain why we feel a certain way about someone if we or they have not taken the time to communicate with us or share how they feel about us. It is awkward; and we do not know how to share platonic love or how to communicate it. Men tend to show their love in a factual manner, without feelings, and women tend to show their love through doing something for the person in a nurturing or caretaking manner.

The media shows and tell us how to communicate erotic love or love making in an intimate setting; however, no one tells or shows us how to show genuine feelings of caring or platonic feelings of love. Have you ever wondered what it would be like to communicate quality and values in your relationship with others? Ask yourself why am I afraid to love? Am I afraid I will lose something of myself or that I will become too vulnerable? You are the only one who can feel your feelings, think your thoughts, and make your choice to feel love or be loving.

How to Communicate Your Quality and Values

Your values determine what's really most important in your life. So, what is most important in your life right now? Your values are the underlying foundational pieces that you've determined to be the most important parts of your life. In other words, it's those standards and principles that you truly stand for. It's what you fight for and take a stand for. It's what you would be willing to risk embarrassment for. It's what you would be willing to speak out for even if the numbers were not in your favor. And it's what you might even be willing to put your life on the line for. So, what is it that you truly value the most? Is it health? Is it family? Is it freedom? Liberty? Or is it love? What is it that you truly value? Find out and live accordingly.

Your priorities are the day-to-day choices you make about the activities you determine to be most important to you. Typically people's priorities are correlated with their values—maybe not exactly, but there is a significant correlation. Your values system will help you to determine what's most important to do every day. And furthermore, your values and priorities will help keep you on the path of your purpose and your vision, because they should all be in alignment with each other. Let me repeat that: Your values on love, your vision for love, and your purpose for being on the planet should all be in alignment with each other, and if love is not one of your core values, you will have a deficit of love feelings for yourself and others.

All people have the unique gift to communicate principles of quality and to share their values. They have the ability to bring people together for a common cause to help them to grow and develop as a team member and work for the common good of a project at hand. Good leaders project charisma, caring feelings, self-confidence, and loving feelings for others. They send a message to others that they can be trusted to take charge of the task at hand to produce a positive outcome, because they care about the feelings and welfare of others. When we do not feel loved, appreciated, or cared about, we will find a way to fill the void or emptiness, and sometimes our need to feel loved will be filled through the use of substances or food. Do you use food to fill a lack of or a void of love? Take the inventory below to find out.

Are You Using Food to Fill the Void of Love or a Meaningful Relationship? Are You an Eating Disorder Codependent?

Use this questionnaire from Fat is a Family Affair to evaluate the extent of your involvement with an under or overeater of food.

Answer each question below for yourself.

What Works When "Diets" Don't?

Do you force yourself to be on diets?

Do you threaten to leave your partner due to weight?

Do you check on your/the diet constantly?

Do you make promises based on pounds lost or gained?

Do you hide food from an over eater?

Do you worry incessantly about an under eater?

Have you "walked on eggshells" so as not to upset the over/undereater?

Do you throw food away so the over eater person won't find it?

Have you excused the erratic, sometimes violent mood swings resulting from sugar binges?

Do you change social activities so the over eater won't be tempted?

Do you manipulate budgets to control spending on food and clothing?

Do you purchase and promote eating the "right" foods?

Do you promote gyms, health spas, and miracle cures?

Do you break into emotional tirades when you catch the over eater bingeing?

Are you constantly disappointed when you see a relapse?

Are you embarrassed by the over/under eater's appearance?

Do you falsely console the over/under eater when he or she is embarrassed?

Have you lowered your expectations of what you might like?

Does your weight fluctuate with your loved one's (you up, he or she down)?

Have you stopped attending to your own grooming?

Do you have many aches and pains or a preoccupation with health?

Are you drinking heavily or using sleeping pills or tranquilizers?

Do you bribe the other person with food?

Do you talk about the eater's body to him or her or to others?

Do you feel, life will be perfect if the over/under eater shaped up?

Are you grateful you aren't "that bad"?

Boundaries

Boundaries are the dividing lines that separate you from others, or where you end and other people begin. This includes understanding what your limits are, what your needs are, and what is unacceptable for you. You can quickly see how your dealmakers and your deal-breakers will help you to define some of your boundaries. This includes being proactive or assertive and asking for what you want. On the other hand, it's also letting people know what you don't want or what is unacceptable for you. If you do this you will create your highest self-respect and self-esteem. We need to know, practice, and learn from our boundaries.

Your boundaries are even more than that. You also have boundaries that you set with yourself. What this means is to set boundaries between different parts of your life, so, for example, you don't become a workaholic. Finding time for your friends, time to exercise, and time just to rest and relax would all be examples of you setting boundaries with yourself so you can have the most balance possible in your life.

In this day and age there is a big invitation out there to get into a workaholic mode of "bigger, better, faster, more, now" which seems to be the paradigm many people and businesses operate from. When you have inner boundaries with yourself and have external boundaries, both together makes for a winning combination. Without boundaries you never know what might happen.

How to Create Boundaries Around Things You Love

It is easier to create boundaries around an object than it is to create boundaries around your feelings and matters of the heart. I suggest you first create boundaries around your money so that your heart cannot be manipulated to separate you from your money. It is easier to start protecting your money so that you will have the practice on how to not let others use your emotions to control your heart strings. It is alright to love money for the things it affords you to have, and the things it affords you to do to help others; however, money can never be a replacement for the love your heart and emotions need and want. Your relationships should never suffer because of the time you spend making money. Money is a tool you need and use to provide for yourself and your family. You need the skills of money making and money saving. However, your love making skills of showing affection, tenderness, compassion, empathy, and sympathy can be useful in getting and keeping money.

These are some of the emotional traits that you want to let go of; Fear, Impatience, Frustration, Envy, Jealousy, Criticism,

Complaining, Anger, and Rage. Confusion and frustration can quickly arise inside us when we feel we won't ever have enough to meet our needs, goals, or desires. Our ego is a desiring machine that is always wanting, wanting. It does not know what is, true heart satisfaction. It is only through your heart that you will find the feeling of being enough and having enough. When you are enough and have enough emotionally it will manifest into your outer experience of having a sense of well-being which will give you the feeling of I am enough, because I know how to create whatever I need including love. The secret to manifesting love is a lot like manifesting anything else you want in your life.

Things That Get in The Way of People Finding the Right Lover or Love Relationship:

1. Not knowing what you're looking for; having unclear expectations.

2. Having a long "grocery list8" of what you want in a relationship and looking for the one person to fill it.

3. Living in fear that you will repeat past experiences.

4. Not healing before starting a new relationship.

5. Women fearing that their biological clock is running out.

6. Men having a fear of starting a family and staying committed.

7. Lowering of standards by older singles, giving up or settling, because they are afraid they will always be alone.

8. Not knowing where to meet other singles with whom you might be compatible.

9. Being too busy to date or cultivate a relationship.

10. Discouragement of not finding someone who meets your expectations.

11. Expectations for sex conflicting with how you feel about the person.

12. Cynicism about women or men.

13. Getting involved too quickly.

14. Not knowing how to start a conversation with a date or potential partner.

15. Having a belief mentality that there are "no good men, no good women".

16. Pressure from family or peers to be coupled.

17. Not having the skills to create a successful relationship.

18. Having a fear of failure around your ability to attract a companion.

19. Fear of rejection that no one would, or could like you.

20. Fear of commitment.

21. Shyness.

22. It is easier to stay single rather than go to the trouble of changing to find the love you want.

Look over this list; find the ones that apply to you, then, discuss them with a Relationship Coach like me. You can call me to get a free 30-minute coaching session to help you refine what you really want in a loving relationship. I can be reached at 619-262-9951 or by Email: ida@thejourneytoselflove.com.

Relationships, the Connection of Us and Others

The quality of your life is the direct result of the quality of your relationships—with your divine source, with yourself, and with others. The fastest way to help improve your relationships is to realign your ego with its true nature to serve as a joyful servant of your soul. If you want to break your old patterns of behavior, you will need to retrain your brain to function in harmony with your true nature of peace and then align your actions with your most deeply held values of love and connection with others. When you are you ready, realign your ego to your inner being (soul), and let it serve as a tool to help you connect with others. Follow these guidelines to have a better relationship connection with others.

* Allow your personal compass of love to keep you on track even when you are in the difficult situations. Love has boundaries and is not abuse.

* Learn how to hone your intuitive sense so you trust yourself and others more easily.

* Compromise can wreak havoc in your relationships; learn how to collaborate.

* Learn how to take action from seeking the truth rather than reacting to fear.

* Find how you can experience everyone and everything as a source of love rather than as a source of conflict.

Love is the place you are coming from; it is your being. You are love. Love is the divine force everywhere, the universal energy, the moving power of life that flows in your own heart.

Love is accepting someone as they are and not trying to change them to be who you want them to be.

Relationships and Chemistry

Linda Marshall, M.Div., Director of Couples Programs for the Relationship Coaching Institute, says, "Love is not an emotion, but a physiological drive that is as powerful as hunger and that phenyl ethylamine (PEA for short) acts as a love drug that stimulates feelings of euphoria during the early stage of a relationship. She quotes that this altered state of infatuation suppresses the part of our brain which is designed to warn and protect us from danger." This helps to explain our euphoria and why we may act like we under the influence of a drug.

Author, anthropology professor, and human behavior researcher, Helen Fisher, Ph.D., is one of the major researchers in the field of interpersonal chemistry. She has studied romantic love in 170 societies and found it to be a universal phenomenon and bears all the basic characteristics of addiction. In her research, she has found that MRI images of the brain reveal that the cognitive area of our brain actually loses blood when we are in love.

Dr. Fisher's research has revealed that there are different hormones driving sex, romance, and attachment, the three most common aspects of love. Fisher reveals that love is not an emotion but a physiological drive as powerful as hunger. Romantic love is actually a basic drive that has evolved for the purposes of mating and reproduction.

Sex

The sex drive is driven by testosterone, a libido-enhancing, energy producing chemical secreted in the testes of males and ovaries of females. On average, men produce about 20 times more testosterone than women. What do you suppose that means for the attraction factor for women? It may explain why some women are slow to take action in starting a romantic encounter.

Romance

In the breathless phase of romantic attraction we are elated, full, and overflowing with energy and obsessed with our love interest, thinking of them almost every waking second and often dreaming of them while we sleep. This is a period of extreme pleasure in which we feel more alive and are more alert, thinking and acting more quickly than usual.

This response is involuntary and enhanced by increased levels of naturally-occurring dopamine and norepinephrine. Novelty of any kind, especially when infatuated in a new relationship, increases levels of these two chemicals in our brains. The elevated activity of these two "love drugs" increases the production of testosterone, linking our attraction to someone with our desire for them sexually. It is a time when sexual tension is overpowering. An interesting phenomenon that occurs simultaneously is a decrease in serotonin, the chemical that eases tension and produces a sensation of relaxation. Our system is truly excited and experiencing a sustained "high".

During this time we focus our attention on our love interest, and everything that occurs between us takes on special meaning. Along with our euphoria commonly comes swings of insecurity and fear that our love interest isn't as interested as we. We develop an emotional dependence upon the other and experience separation anxiety when not in their presence. Our craving for emotional union is intense and difficult to control. We can become possessive as we guard our lover from the intrusion of any outside threat. We are protecting life's greatest prize—a mating partner.

Fisher states that in general, men are more visually stimulated because their brains are wired to accommodate their search for a woman to give them healthy babies, while the memory part of a woman's brain is wired to accommodate her need to find a man who keeps his promises. And thus this ensures the survival of our species.

Attachment

Love changes over time. Eventually the euphoria subsides as we settle into the next phase, attachment, characterized by feelings of security and calm. At this point, oxytocin and vasopressin are the chemicals at play in our bodies. Oxytocin is released during orgasm in both the male and the female. In the brain, both these chemicals are involved in social behavior and bonding. Researchers believe these chemicals are in play in supporting the formation of trust between two people and the bond they experience during sexual activity.

The Four Basic Personality Types

Dr. Fisher is the guiding force behind the matching technology of the online dating service, Chemistry.com. It has long been known that we tend to be attracted to people similar to ourselves—with the same ethnic, social, religious, educational, and economic background. This also extends to our attraction to people with a similar amount of physical attractiveness, a comparable intelligence, and parallel attitudes, expectations, values, and interests.

What is only beginning to be known is that the chemicals in our bodies affect our personalities. Dr. Fisher has identified four personality styles that accompany the characteristic dominant level of one of four hormones: dopamine, serotonin, estrogen, and testosterone. These personality styles are also predictive of whom we are more likely to be attracted.

Higher Dopamine = "Explorer"

Someone with high levels of dopamine Fisher calls an "Explorer". What makes an explorer a desirable partner is their high energy, high creativity, and spontaneity. They tend to be artistic and seek novelty, risk, and pleasure. They are intellectually curious and not easily swayed by the opinions of others. The challenges in relating to an explorer are their propensity toward addiction and their tendency to philander.

Higher Serotonin = "Builder"

Someone with high levels of serotonin Fisher calls a "Builder". What makes a builder a desirable partner is their calm demeanor and low anxiety. They have a deep attachment to their home and family and are often consistent, loyal, and protective of those they love. They have managerial skills, are sympathetic, and cooperative. They work hard and have a lot of common sense. Their patience gives them the ability to complete detailed, painstaking jobs more easily than most people. The challenge in relating to a builder is their propensity to be "right" and to know the "right way" to do things.

Higher Estrogen = "Negotiator"

Someone with high levels of estrogen Fisher calls a "Negotiator". What makes a negotiator a desirable partner is their idealistic, big picture thinking. They are relational, egalitarian, non-hierarchical, intuitive, flexible, and excel at long-term planning and consensus building. They usually have high verbal and social skills, tending to be networkers who are imaginative, capable of deep empathy, and nurturing. The challenge in relating to a negotiator is their absolute need to establish a deep connection with you.

Higher Testosterone = "Director"

Someone with high levels of testosterone she calls a "Director". What makes a director a desirable partner is their daring, originality, directness, and inventiveness. They usually are good leaders who are conscious of rank and appropriate behavior. Achieving positions of power and influence often comes easily to them. They can be very assertive and tough minded, focusing on schedules, rules, and routines. They tend to be competitive and efficient. As an independent thinker, they are skilled at abstract thinking and short-term planning. The challenge in relating to a director is their mental inflexibility and limited social sensitivity.

According to Dr. Fisher, Builders are best matched with Explorers, and Directors are best matched with Negotiators. Negotiators, with their flexibility, empathy, and nurturing abilities, are compatible and sought after by all the other personality styles. There is little published information about these personality types at this time.

Conscious Mating

Conscious Mating requires that we understand what motivates us, what we are feeling, and why we are feeling it. We are complex creatures driven by primal biological forces as well as our higher cognitive abilities. All successful relationships depend upon our ability to make good long-term partner choices; and understanding the chemistry of love enables us to balance our heart with our head.

The Journey to Find Love or Be Loved

As you continue on your journey to find the lover of your life, there are other things you want to keep in mind. Clean up your living space. It is hard to attract a new love or lover into your life when there is a lot of clutter in your mind or your life. This may sound weird, but cleaning up your living space will help you in your pursuit of love. Consider looking at your physical space from the perspective of someone seeing it for the first time. What does your living space say about you? Does it feel inviting? Warm? Cozy? Or does it feel more like a bachelor/ette crash pad where you store your dirty laundry?

Ask a friend for their opinion on this. Your living space is an outward reflection of your inner life. Consider what your living space says to others who are on the outside looking in? I find that when I straighten up my living space and clear out my clutter, I'm better able to focus more on the important things, like nurturing a love interest or getting excited about the idea of meeting new people or finding a new lover or love.

I just got rid of some old books and papers of 10 years ago, and I was surprised how energized I felt getting rid of my clutter. There were some old feelings and emotions that I had to let go of to move on, and to accept that I did the best I could under the circumstances with the information and knowledge I had at the time. I am more emotionally mature now, so I do not take things as personally. Neither do I feel mortally wounded by what has happened to me like I used to feel. Life has a way of forcing us to live with the pain and agony of our past or to turn the page of our life to a new chapter in our relationships to see the possibility of a new lover or a new platonic friendship or relationship. There are many traps in dating to find a new love relationship. Use the following checklist to identify possible red flags in a prospective relationship you may be considering.

Conscious Dating Red Flags

Your Name   Potential Partner

Date   **Y or N**

1. Would I want to spend the rest of my life with this person exactly as they are?

2. Would I want this person to raise my child?

3. Would I want my child to be exactly like this person?

4. Do I want to rescue or "help" them because I see their potential?

5. I love the way they look or their status, and it builds my self-esteem to be with them.

6. We have some things in common and so I'm avoiding looking at glaring differences.

7. They appear to be totally different than people I've been with in the past.

8. I'm focusing on one important quality (money, sex, fun, humor, etc.) and ignoring unmet requirements.

9. Reacts to frustration with anger, rage, blame.

10. Blames others or circumstances for life situation.

11. Tries to control everything, including me.

12. Immature, impulsive, and/or irresponsible.

13. Emotionally distant or void, aloof.

14. Still pining for a past relationship.

15. Someone who wants me to make their sad life better.

---

16. Married or otherwise unavailable to commit to me.

17. Active addiction, addictive behavior (rationalized as "not a problem").

18. Is pessimistic and negative about things that matter to the man.

19. Lacks integrity in dealing with people, money, etc.

20. Judgmental attitude toward themselves and others.

21. Unwilling to self-examine, accept feedback, take responsibility.

22. Doesn't keep agreements.

23. What she/he says about him/herself doesn't match reality.

24. Emotional roller coaster, recurring, or regular emotional drama.

25. This isn't what I really want, but I don't want to be alone.

26. Changeable, inconsistent behavior.

27. Inability to listen.

28. I notice myself trying to change this person to fit what I want, instead of accepting them for who they are.

29. Talks too much (especially about self), monopolizes conversation.

30. Overly quiet, withdrawn.

Total the checked items. Circle the ones that need close attention, decision-making, or require more information.

On a scale from 0 (Not at all) to 100 (Perfect fit) my minimum score for considering any relationship is _____

Using the above scale I score this potential relationship _____.

Based upon the above results, I should proceed dating this potential partner. Y   N

I should not proceed dating this potential partner. Y   N

If it's clear you should not proceed dating this potential partner and you have any difficulty moving on, show this checklist to your best friend, close family member, therapist, or coach and get the support you need.

The Secret to Manifesting Love

The secret to manifesting enough love is to soak and rest in the feeling of love throughout your day that "**you**" are enough. When you realize this, everything changes. You naturally start creating abundant feelings about your love situation which is supported by your positive empowering beliefs about love. The truth is that no matter how much love you have, your ego will never ever feel that it is enough. We will never feel that we are adequate. We all have feelings of self-doubt about whether we are pretty enough, tall enough, have the right body size, hips, breast, or bra size, right lip thickness or curve, right dress size, the skin tone or color, the right hair length, color, or thickness. We are obsessed with the question: Am I enough to attract the man/woman of my dreams? It is only when you meditate on and connect with your spiritual inner self that you will be able to see the beauty inside you, and when you see your inner beauty everyone will see it as well.

Your feelings of love deprivation and your feelings of being alone and without love will loom big in your life as long as you see this as a problem. Anything that we focus on will become bigger in our life, be it lack of love, lack of attention, being overly shy, or not knowing how to make friends. It will all become a bigger problem, the more we see it a problem without a solution. We must give others the freedom to like us or to not like us, to love us or to not love us. Do not become attached to or resist being liked or loved by someone else. People will either like you or not like you. They will either love you or not love you, and you have no control over it. Strive to like yourself and become a likable or loving human being who deserves to be loved for being who you are. Learn to be at peace with yourself with or without a man/woman or having someone love you.

When you start thinking, feeling, and vibrating like a lover, you will become more attractive to others. The key is to be in a constant state of acceptance and gratitude for who you are. See and know that you are the essence of love at the core of your being. Being with this feeling and knowing is a spiritual awakening experience. Sit in the core of the feeling of love on a daily basis. Take a step back and observe any judgments that arise inside you without getting entangled in your story about how love should look or how love should show up in your life. Just be with the feeling of the absence of love until it passes or until you feel comfortable in letting it be or allowing yourself to not have love or be loved every second of the day. Eventually the tension you feel and your fears around Love will fade away and you will feel a release inside you that lifts you to a higher vibration, and a lighter feeling of love will begin to expand inside you.

Chapter 3

The Pillars of a Good Relationship

The best kind of relationships are those that give you a sense of wholeness, security, safety, and a feeling that you are nourished, cared for, and thought of. Where there is even exchange of giving and receiving energy. Sometimes out of our desperation to be loved, we latch on to people whose words do not match their actions. Love is a verb, an "action". Remember to watch what people do, not what they say. Beautiful words stated by the wrong person will bring you heartache and grief. Love is a giving activity. There are many people who will say they love you, who have no idea of what love is, or know how to give love. It is because they themselves have never received love, therefore are void of love, or they are "users" who only know how to take, but not give of their energy, time, attention, caring, or concern. Everything is all them. They are "Me" parasites who only wants to devour their victims, which causes undue suffering and emotional pain.

Suffering occurs when you become attached to expecting more in a relationship than what would give you true happiness. Suffering can be the same in the work you do or in the relationships you have. What makes you sufficiently happy in work is having an opportunity to do work that you enjoy doing. What makes you sufficiently happy in relationships is having an opportunity to love and relate with those you love. Focusing on doing work you enjoy will lead to success and abundance. Focusing on being happy with others and experiencing your love for them when there is an opportunity to do so, will lead you to find those who love you as you are. Happiness is found in enjoying what shows up in your space in the moment. It is the path of least resistance, and it is the path to move through life with ease, peace, and harmony.

You do not hurt a love that loves you and you do not love a love that hurts you. If loving a person makes you happy, it is the right person to love. If loving a person gives you more suffering than joy, it is the wrong person to love. Divine love can and should be given to everyone. Personal love is a sacred thing that is not to be given away to the wrong person or in the wrong place. When love is given to the wrong person or in the wrong place, it contracts and becomes repressed. When love is given to the right person in the right place, love expands and multiplies. Love should bring you joy, contentment, ease, comfort, happiness, and fun as you give and receive from the other person or thing.

What are you looking for when you say you want love? Are you looking for?

• Support (Trust)

• Acceptance (Recognition)

• Validation (Self-Worth)

• Nurturance (Needed)

• Self-Esteem (Feeling of Importance)

• Self-Appreciation (Approval)

• Security (Provided for/Survival)

• Spiritual Wellness (Connected to a Power greater than you)

• Happier Relationships (Connections)

• The validation you have always wanted and never received

• The lover you never had and ache to have

How to Find Love, Inside Oneself

The law of the universe is love. We are made perfect in this law when we enter into conscious communion with the object of our love. Love is the fulfillment of the law; that is, it is only through love that the law of the universe can fulfill itself in your experience, because love harmonizes and unifies everything. Love gives itself to everything, because it flows through everything. We can never be without love for the very essence of who are is love.

Love does not hurt us; neither does it make us feel bad. And if a person loves us, they share the love inside themselves with us. They will radiate a warm glow of peace and tranquility from the inner core of their being. Love does not hurt us, nor does it abuse us. Love is about freedom, peace, joy, and happiness.

People who love themselves are secure within themselves, and they have a reservoir of loving energy to share. They are not stingy with their love, because they realize that love springs forth from them in a never ending fountain of inner well-being. It is a love from the Divine impulse of the universe that keeps replenishing itself on an hourly basis inside us.

LOVE

Unknown

Love enough and love will give you wings;
it will cushion the rough places in your road, ease the strains of life,
straightening the way before you, to make effortless the tasks,
erasing the drudgery,
Replace it with pleasantness.
Refuse to harbor any feeling other than love.
Your body cannot be out of ease, diseased, while love fills your
mind and heart.

You will be fearless for perfect love casts out fear.

You will be happy, for disharmony cannot enter where love is.

You will become beloved, for like attracts like, and love is the greatest attracting power.

You will never be lonely, for love peoples your world with loving companions.

You will never be sad, for love is the greatest happiness maker.

You will be alive, alert, and aware, for love sharpens all faculties.

You will be successful, for love never fails.

Love with every atom of your energy, and no other task will be required of you.

Fill your mind and heart with love to overflowing, and life will pour out its richest blessings upon you.

Love does not consist in gazing at each other, but in looking outward together in the same direction.

Learn To Live the Life You Desire and Deserve

You can program your subconscious mind to create the life you desire and deserve. Each and every moment of your day there is abundant opportunity for you to move from a place of yearning to a place of love, deserving, and abundance. The tools you use to create better outcomes in your life are the same tools you have been using all your life: they are: language, imagination, and emotion.

Whatever your mind is focused on—both consciously and unconsciously—is the reality you create for yourself and those around you. Yet, most of the time, you are programming the subconscious 90% of your mind to create a life that is unfulfilling, that lacks choices, and is filled with pained communication.

Your language directs your thinking. Whatever you are contemplating or thinking you create more of. Through language, we create our own personal Heaven or Hell. If your internal dialogue is, "I'm not good enough. I'm a fool. I did this wrong. My Mom said that about me, and I believe it's the truth!" you will create a reality based on this dialogue. Your subconscious mind does not discriminate. And the outside world will give you evidence of whatever it is your subconscious mind is asking for.

In the privacy of your home, you can learn how to recognize and correct the language patterns—both your internal self-talk and external communication with others—that have been holding you back. By changing the language of your mind, you change the reality of your past, present, and future.

Everyone has the ability to do this. Anyone can learn, because my approach is holistic and personal. My self-help products will teach you proven methods for finding the love, joy, prosperity, and lasting spiritual wellness you have been seeking but did not know how to achieve.

All world religions say that man and woman are made in the image and likeness of Spirit. Cultures from around the world agree that whatever this power is, it is creative in nature. This presupposes that we, too, are creative by nature, as we are made in the image and likeness of this power. Now, my big question to you is, do you think it would be worthwhile to find out how you actually create? NLP is the quickest way to program the most infinite power on the planet: your own human mind.

Dr. Steven Covey says you should ask four questions of yourself:

What is it that I am really good at?

What is it I really love to do?

What need, can I serve for someone?

What is life asking of me?

When have you tapped into your mind and your talent, you'll discover what you're good at. Your heart is your passion (what you love doing). The physical side is your economic need that you're serving in society and this drives your economic engine. And your spiritual side has to do with what does your conscience tells you to do in a given circumstance or situation.

If you can overlap those four things, I feel you can find your inner voice. My experience with most entrepreneurs is that they have found their voice in that way, although sometimes they have not. Sometimes they're beleaguered and beat up. I think that they are so turned on, but the problem is they don't often surround themselves with people who think differently. These people can compensate for their weakness to where they appreciate their voice, so that they create kind of a harmonious chorus, as it were, of people who really know how to work together in the use of their voices.

How to Find a Relationship That Is Right for You

If you are not in the relationship of your choice it may be that you have unresolved issues related to the following concerns.

Write down your answer to the following questions. What is your relationship like with men/women? Are you just barely on speaking terms or are you best friends with him/her? Many people have unhealthy relationships with men/women that hold them back from manifesting the kind of intimacy they seek and deserve, is this your problem. Imagine for a few moments that you can see, feel and experience your ideal partner. What would this person look like? How old are they, what kind of work are they doing? What kinds of things do the two of you have in common, your likes and dislikes? How are you treating this person and how are/do they treat you? Are you needy or demanding in any way? Do you think, "I have to have more of you", or "I'm never going to see enough of you?" Do you feel secure, or loved by them? Do you trust women/ men? Do you trust that they will always be there when you need them?

Can you imagine that you are best friends with him/her? What would this relationship look like? One important element of being someone's best friend is trust. Do you trust that this person is going to be there for you when you need them, and that they will do whatever they can to support you? When someone is your best friend, you know that you can relax when you think about them because you know they will always be there for you. When you can truly relax with them you'll see that they always support you no matter what occurs in your life. This element of trust shifts your vibration and allows for more love and intimacy to pour into your relationship.

Secondly, when you are best friends with someone, you truly respect, honor and appreciate them for what who they are. You don't try to change them, and you always focus on what you appreciate about them instead of what you dislike. See yourself now walking hand-in-hand with this person. See them at your side, supporting you and providing for you so that you can experience the joys and growing opportunities of what a juicy love life looks. Are they just like a best friend? Does feel good to have them around? Take a moment right now and open up your heart to a healthy abundant, loving, committed relationship with yourself and others. Is it O.K. for you to really like or love them? Use your imagination, and see what this looks or feel like. Imagine having a loving kind relationship in your life. If any negative thoughts about men or women come, just say "cancel, cancel, cancel", and refocus on what a trusting healthy abundant relationship would look like. Now relax your thoughts and get into the knowing that the perfect relationship will always be there for you no matter what.

A Credo For Your Relationship With Others

Thomas Gordon, Ph. D

You and I are in a relationship which I value and want to keep. Yet each of us is a separate person with his/her own unique needs and the right to meet those needs. When you are having problems meeting your needs, I will try to listen with genuine acceptance in order to facilitate your finding your own solutions instead of depending on mine. I also will try to respect your right to choose your own beliefs and develop your own values, different though they may be from mine.

However, when your behavior interferes with what I must do to get my own needs met, I will openly and honestly tell you how your behavior affects me, trusting that you respect my needs and feelings enough to try to change the behavior that is unacceptable to me. Also, whenever some behavior of mine is unacceptable to you, I hope you will openly and honestly tell me your feelings. I will then listen and try to change my behavior.

At those times when we find that either of us cannot change his/her behavior to meet the other's needs, let us acknowledge that we have a conflict-of-needs that requires resolving. Let us then commit ourselves to resolve each such conflict without either of us resorting to the use of power or authority to try to win at the expense of the other losing. I respect your needs, but I also must respect my own. So let us always strive to search for a solution that will be acceptable to both of us. Your needs will be met, but so will mine— neither will lose, both will win.

In this way, you can continue to develop as a person through satisfying your needs, but so can I. Thus, ours can be a healthy relationship in which each of us can strive to become what he/she is capable of being. And we continue to relate to each other with mutual respect, love, and peace.

Goals for Improving Your Relationship

If you have decided to stay and work on a relationship that is difficult—even painful or abusive—then it is important to be clear about what needs to change and how you plan to make those changes happen. A couple of things to keep in mind:

• You cannot make your partner change. You can let your partner know what changes you plan to make and what changes you would like him/her to make, but it is up to your partner to decide whether he/she will change or not.

• You are not responsible for your partner's actions. If your partner is abusive, changing your behavior will not make the abuse stop.

Start with listing what you've tried that has **not** worked to improve your relationship in the past.

_____

_____

_____

_____

Now list what has worked to improve the relationship in the past.

_____

_____

_____

_____

What are the things that must change in order for you to continue this relationship?

_____

_____

_____

Now set a goal for those changes to happen:

_____

_____

_____

_____

Who is responsible for making this goal happen? How?

_____

_____

_____

What are the steps that will need to be taken to achieve this goal?

_____

_____

_____

When will you reevaluate this goal to see if it has been achieved?

_____

_____

_____

What will happen if the goal is reached?

_____

_____

_____

Areas of Conflict in Communicating as a Couple

This information is designed for couples who are committed to their relationships and interested in improving the quality of their interaction. Some common areas of conflict in couple communications are:

1. How to talk about your problems and feelings without arousing your partner's anger or defensiveness.

2. How to listen to your partner's problems and feelings without becoming angry and defensive yourself.

3. How to resolve conflicts when both you and your partner have talked and listened and find you disagree.

4. How to handle anger constructively and prevent arguments from escalating.

Communication Conflict, Between Men and Women

Saying exactly what you are thinking and feeling all the time is **not** a leading trait that makes for a great communicator; or even a good one. Being in touch with your feelings is good. But throwing them out when they come to you, to not "filter" them and putting no conscious thought behind how the other person will hear and receive your words can be counterproductive.

Many women spend days, weeks, or months analyzing, processing, and discussing a thought or idea they have about a man or about their relationship.

Then, they come to a conclusion and present their thoughts to their guy. And then what happens? Most of the time the woman expects the man to listen and **very quickly** understand what she is saying, what it means about their relationship; how it makes her feel and why she feels this way.

This often does not work out well, because the man has not had the benefit of the time for discussion and analysis the woman has had. The woman may have been expecting her communication to give the man a perfect view and experience of what it is like to be her, however since the man has not has the time to research his or her thoughts he will be at a disadvantage. The man may see things differently and may have his own perspective of the situation.

The challenge many women have with men is that it is very difficult to know what is going on with a man because he will rarely, come out and say exactly how he is thinking or feeling. Most men do not routinely take the time to examine what they are feeling and why they feel what they feel as do most women.

How to Communicate With a Partner

A lot of couples begin a communication program or class with both secretly (and not so secretly) believing that their problems are caused in large part by their partners. Each person sees himself or herself as the mostly innocent victim of the other person's bad behavior, and each person hopes that the class will get the partner to change: to listen, to express feelings, or to stop nagging and criticizing.

Because this is a common expectation, I want to emphasize what a communication class can and can't provide. Neither the class nor you can change your partner. Who you *can* change is *yourself*: how you behave, how you communicate, and how you solve problems. As you wonder how to get your relationship to change, you realize that you hold one of the most important keys:

Your own behavior. You are incredibly powerful influence on your relationship.

You may say, "I have tried to change myself and it didn't work. It's about time for my partner to do some changing." That may well be true, but the fact remains that the most effective way to bring about change in a relationship is to change yourself. Both of you need to swallow your pride, to take the first step, and take the attitude: "I'm going to learn these skills; I'm going to respond differently." Even if it occasionally feels like giving in to the other person, the formal research with couples has shown that it is in your personal self-interest, not just for the good of the relationship, to learn these skills for yourself.

Some Communication Patterns to Recognize and Avoid

1. The Summarizing Self Syndrome

Both people keep restating their own positions. Nobody listens to anyone else. The conversation sounds like this:

" Blah, blah."

"Yak, yak."

"What I said was blah, blah."

"Didn't you hear me say yak. Yak?"….and so on.

2. Kitchen Sink-ing

People start out discussing one issue but then drift into other topics. They often end up dragging "everything but the kitchen sick" into the conversation. Pretty soon both people get the feeling that they have to deal with all of the issues at once.

3. Yes, But…..

Every time one person makes a suggestion, the other person finds something wrong with it. Partners sometimes are not aware of this habit.

4. Cross Complaining

Person A makes a complaint or request of person B. Person B doesn't respond to the issue; instead, B brings up a complaint about A.

5. Mind Reading

One person assumes knowledge of what the other person is "really" thinking or wanting.

6. Interrupting

Not allowing the person to express their opinion.

7. Insulting Your Partner

Saying demeaning or unkind words

8. Threatening Your Partner

Making the person feel scared or that their life is in danger.

9. Airing Old Resentments

Bringing up old hurts or resentments from the past

10. Being Vague

People speak in generalities without giving specifics. For example, "You're driving funny today."

11. **Over-generalizing-**These statements usually begin with "You never…" or "You always…"

Assumptions and Skills for Effective Communication

The first basic assumption is that feelings, ***all kinds of feelings exist***. Feelings are not good or bad, wrong or right, correct or incorrect, they are just feelings. The second assumption is that all of us have the right to have any feeling in the world. Some behaviors or actions may need to be limited, but *any feeling* is okay. And each of us is the *ultimate authority* on our own feelings.

No one can tell you what you feel or don't feel. Another person may not like what you are feeling or may feel differently. But no one can tell you that you don't feel the way you do. The third assumption is that an intimate relationship, at its best, is a place where both partners feel safe to share feelings, when they choose to, without getting attacked for doing so. To build that kind of relationship, you need two sets of communications skills. One set is *speaking*, and one is for *listening.* Both skills are essential.

Skills for Speaking

Use "I-messages". An "I" message is a sentence that starts with the word "I" and expresses a feeling. Here is why an "I-message" is more effective than a "you-message". Suppose X says to Y, "You play too much golf." Y can protest, "I do not." Y feels attacked and put down and is tempted to retaliate with a counterattack. But if X says to Y, "I feel jealous when you play golf," Y cannot say, "You do not." X is taking responsibility for his/her own feelings, and no one can say that X doesn't, or shouldn't, fell that way.

To communicate what you are feeling, you need to *know* what you are feeling. This takes practice. It involves getting to know your body and the signals it gives to tell you what you are feeling. It also involves becoming familiar with the typical pattern of thoughts that go along with specific feelings for you. To help you start this process, use the sample feeling chart below. When you want to know what you are feeling, you might look at the chart and select the word that best approximates how you feel at the moment

Positive

Willing	Content	Turned on	Calm
Secure	Loving	Ready	Warm
Strong	Bubbly	Interested	Sexy
Happy	Peaceful	Ambitious	Excited
Busy	Confident	Imaginative	

I feel....

A Little	**Somewhat**	**Very**......	
Negative			
Grouchy	Ashamed	Silly	Sorry
Sad	Bored	Hurt	Sully
Anxious	Alone	Shy	Rebellious
Tired	Dumb	Guilty	Confused
Nervous	Trapped	Frustrated	Listless
Restless	Put down	Ignored	Depressed

When you speak in I-statements, you don't have to use complicated feeling words. Someone once said that there are four basic feelings, and three of them rhyme: mad, sad, glad, and afraid.

If you're ever not sure what you're feeling, scan those four. Other useful feeling phrases are:

I like it when ....

I don't like it when...

I want....

I wish....

Sometimes our feelings have two parts; for example, "*I want* to go, but I *don't want* to spend the money." This is a perfectly legitimate I-statement, so when you feel two things, say both of them.

Other Do's and Don'ts for Effective Speaking:

Do own your feelings. For example, "I get mad."

Do be specific when you feel that way. For example, "I get mad when clothes are on the bathroom floor."

Do say directly what you want. For example: "I'd like you to take them out of the bathroom."

Don't ask questions.

Don't judge, preach, criticize, or blame.

Don't use name calling.

Don't interpret, diagnose, or analyze.

Here is a formula you can use to build an I-message when you want to give your partner feedback about his/her behavior.

> "When you do....X... (Describe the behavior), I feel...Y."
>
> And if you want change, add:
>
> "I would prefer...Z." (Describe the behavior)

Relationship Skills for Listening to Others

Your partner's I-messages are wasted if you don't hear them. Therefore, good communication requires using a skill called **validating** or **active listening**. Active listening means *hearing* your partner and communicating to him/her that if you are seeing things his/her way, with his/her assumptions, it would be reasonable to feel that way.

The essence of active listening is to express empathy with your partner's feelings, while preserving a neutral, non-judgmental stance yourself. It is not necessary to share or agree with your partner's feelings in order to empathize with them. It is also not necessary to solve his or her problem or to offer advice or suggestions.

In active listening you paraphrase the content and reflect back the feeling or meaning behind your partner's words. This shows your partner that his/her feelings are heard and understood.

It encourages your partner to make his/her own I-statements, and it thereby sets the stage for later negotiations. It also tends to defuse your partner's opposition and to create a positive, caring atmosphere.

Other Do's and Don'ts for Effective Listening Validation:

Do remember the basic assumption that every person has the right to any feeling in the world.

Do put your own feelings "on a back burner" while you are the "listener". Later, when you are the "speaker", you will have a chance to express your feelings, and your partner will listen to you.

Don't say or imply that your partner "shouldn't feel that way". Don't express your feelings—of disagreement or agreement—or make suggestions at this point.

Don't interpret what you think your partner "really feels". Don't try to get your partner to change his or her mind.

Some Examples of Active Listening

"It sounds like you want it too but are worried about how we'll be able to pay for it."

"What I'm hearing you say is that my not checking with you first caused you a lot of embarrassment."

"Your first choices are to go out for pizza, second choice is to grill hamburgers at home, and you really don't want to go out for chicken. Did I get that right?"

"Let me check out if I'm hearing you accurately. What you minded wasn't so much that the house was dirty, but you felt that I didn't care enough to clean it.'

"You're saying you really like it when we snuggle up on the sofa."

How To Listen To Hear

When I ask you to listen to me and you start giving advice you have not done what I asked.

When I ask you to listen to me and you begin to tell me why I shouldn't feel that way, you are trampling on my feelings.

When I ask you to listen to me and you feel you have to do something to solve my problem, you have failed me, strange as that may seem.

Listen! All I asked was that you listen. Not to talk or do—just hear me.

Advice is cheap: 10 cents will get you both Dear Abby and Billy Graham in the same newspaper.

And I can do for myself; I'm not helpless, maybe discouraged and faltering, but not helpless.

When you do something for me that I can and need to do for myself, you contribute to my fear and weakness.

But, when you accept as a simple fact that I do feel what I feel, no matter how irrational, then I can quit trying to convince you and can get about the business of understanding what's behind this irrational feeling. And when that's clear, the answers are obvious and I don't need advice.

Irrational feelings make sense when we understand what is behind them.

Perhaps that's why prayer works, sometimes, for some people because Spirit is mute, and He doesn't give advice or try to fix things. "They" just listen and let you work it out for yourself.

So, please listen and just hear me. And, if you want to talk, wait a minute for your turn and I will listen to you.

Anon

Soft Assertion Skills

"Soft assertion" means speaking up about your warm, positive feelings toward each other. It is dangerous to assume that your spouse knows you appreciate him/her when he/she does something special. Say It. Even routine behaviors are more likely to happen again if they are acknowledged.

Rules to Follow:

Be as specific as you can in acknowledging positive behavior.

1. Describe, don't evaluate, for example: Do say: "The spaghetti is delicious tonight."

Don't say, "You're such a wonderful cook."

2. Avoid global generalizations of all kinds such as, "You, always do such a great job," "I can always count on you," etc. (These

statements are often embarrassing to the recipient and are usually discounted.)

3. Acknowledge attempts and/or partially completed tasks by commenting on what is done well. Don't wait for perfection or total success.

4. Even if it seems obvious, **SAY IT!** One kind word produces another. You'll be surprised how fast a positive cycle can be generated and what far-reaching effects it can have on the whole relationship.

5. When you receive a compliment, say "THANK YOU." Don't apologize or disqualify it.

Do This to Ask For a Request For Change

A request for change should be:

> 1. Positive
>
> 2. Specific
>
> 3. Small
>
> 4. Not the subject of a recent conflict

Examples: Do not say, "I wish you'd quit being such a slob." (Negative and general) "I wish you'd be neater." (Positive, but too vague)

Do say, "I'd really appreciate it if you'd hang up your towel after you use it." (Positive, specific, and small)

Essential Relationship Skills In Every Area of Your Life

The skills you need to develop or improve your relationships are often a test to determine if you are ready for success in your relationships with others.

  1. Know what you want (intention).

  2. People connections strengthen your personality.

  3. Know your personal strengths and weaknesses.

  4. Get a good supporting network of quality friends

  5. Have relationship goals for yourself

  6. Have an action plan to accomplish your relationship goals, who you want to meet, what character traits you have/want to match, and when do you want this to happen?

  7. Be willing to state your relationship non negotiation rules

Impediments to Collaborate or Connect with Others:

1. Fear of connection

2. Fear of commitment/Impatience.

3. Fear of Rejection

Your Ideal Lover/Partner Traits and Qualities

Much of the time a Partner/Committed Lover:

  _____ Is Nurturing

  _____ Is Flexible

  _____ Is Understanding

_____ Is Consistent

_____ Allows Growth

_____ Acknowledges you as a unique individual

_____ Accepts and approves of who you are, and does not want to change you or make you over to be the person they want

_____ Is Attentive

_____ Wants to Be Involved in Your Life

_____ Open to Guidance/Corrective Feedback

_____ Open to Have Better Communication

_____ Comfortable with Your Faults and Flaws

_____ Can Give Validation

_____ Is Flexible

_____ Value Personal Growth

_____ Is Cooperative

_____ Listens without judgment

_____ Is accepting

_____ Is Kind and Considerate

_____ Knows how to let go (is not possessive)

_____ Establishes and maintains routines as needed

_____ Is an ally/Friend

_____ Models wholeness and balance

_____ Knows the difference between love and non-love touching

_____ Appreciate Consistency

_____ Likes Structure

_____ Gives Positive Reinforcement

_____ Builds Confidence in the other person

_____ Has Realistic Expectations

_____ Is Lovable

_____ Has Good Coping Skills

_____ Is Hopeful, Has a Positive Outlook on the Relationship/Life

_____ Is Trusting and Trust -Worthy

_____ Makes times for Their Partner and their Relationship

_____ Has His or Her Frustrations, Irritations and Anger Under Control most of the time

Check through this list and check which ones you see in your current partner or check the ones you have seen in a partner you dated in the past. Which ones of the traits will you look for in a future partner?

> *"If love be not the law of our being,*
> *the whole of my arguments*
> *falls to pieces."*
> ~ Gandhi

Dr. Ida Greene, PhD

Chapter 4

How Your Family Communication Patterns Affect Your Relationship

Our past is always with us even though we modify it with what happens in the present. As I have mentioned, old thought patterns can continue to produce results even though we are no longer thinking them. By the same token, we can still be acting out old relationships even though these people are not present. These truths are revealed to me over and over again when I take a client's sexual history. When I ask that person to describe his/her first childhood sex experience, I see that the conclusions made right after that experience are often still producing results years and years later. And yet, you do not have to stay stuck in the past. If you change the generalizations now that you made in the past, you can, in effect, change the past.

Since we carry our mind with us wherever we go and we produce the same results over and over, it is obvious that it is only when we change our consciousness that we can expect permanent replacements of old negative patterns. This is why affirmations are so powerful. Try repeating some of these to change your frame of mind

My bedroom is no longer a place of punishment. It is a place of reward.

I now forgive my father/mother for hitting, beating, hurting me. Other men are not my father, and I do not need to fear them.

For the first time in my life I will begin to spend some time relaxing in my bedroom. I have redecorated it in a sensual, cheerful manner and put fresh flowers by my bed.

I now have conversations with my old unfriendly thoughts about men, and I am ready to let go of my fear of being around or with a man.

Affirmations Regarding Negative Past Experiences

1. I forgive myself for _____ (fill in particular negative past experience).

2. I am now free of the past regarding my emotionally negative sexual experiences. I now focus on the value I learned from them.

3. I no longer focus on the losses I have suffered in the past. Instead, I hold on to those things that are of value to me.

4. My early painful sexual experiences do not make me a failure in sex.

5. Since I am responsible for my actions, I do not need to feel guilty about anything.

6. I now forgive women for their ignorant behavior toward me. I am no longer angry at women. I feel loving toward all people. I do not need to get even with women any longer; I can let them love me.

7. I now forgive men for their ignorant behavior toward me. I am no longer angry at men. I feel loving toward them. I do not need to get even with men any longer. I can let them love me.

8. My bedroom and bed is a safe and pleasurable place to be.

9. My bedroom is no longer a place of punishment, deprivation, or restriction. It is a reward, a place for rest, relaxation, pleasure, and inspiration.

Love Is the Only Answer

What is your story about why you do not have love in your life?

What are you committed to be, do, or have in relation to love?

New Insights I Have About Myself

What have you learned about yourself since reading this book so far?

1. My self-esteem/self-worth is now better...

_____

_____

2. I feel deserving because...

_____

3. I am handling my disappointments about...

_____

4. Life is a constant reaching out to learn and grow; "I have grown in the following ways"...

_____

_____

5. Do you have a victim mindset? If so, are you willing to give up this role?

6. Are you grieving about someone or something?

7. Are you willing to let go past hurts and disappointments?

Love is the Only Way to Eliminate Negativity From Your Life

Write down all the people or things in your life that have affected you negatively:

1.

2.

3.

I find that there are basically two types of love in this world: real love and false love. Real love has a quality about it that makes our hearts instantly open and relax. There's a spiritual energy about real love that feels like we all have an infinite amount of time, joy, and energy to give away. Real love is the most healing feeling we can have. It has an abundance of trusting energy and an exquisite sensation of accepting everything in our lives. Real love gives everything of itself to life, never holding back. It gives fully without conditions, always thinking "How can I help?" instead of thinking "What's in it for me?"

False love, on the other hand, wants to be like real love, yet it has an egoist mask it is hiding behind. This mask can only think in terms of "What's in it for me?" and believes that this approach will give it happiness in the end. It chooses to help others out of duty, a feeling of "I have to", or an obligation. It believes that it is doing the right thing, yet is blind to the fact that through obligation it's not actually enjoying its life. This false ego-based love is missing out on a more honest, vulnerable, and selfless approach. It has nothing to do with generosity, appreciation, or real giving. It's energy comes from scheming, planning, wanting, wishing, and hoping that it manifests what it wants. It can only think about its own needs instead of what's best for the whole.

Deep down inside, all this false love wants is to find the source of real love. It's tired of being a fake and wants what is real and true. It's ready to stop hiding behind fear, insecurity, and selfishness. It wants to be free from constantly feeling less than enough. This false love means well, yet its mask unknowingly creates more feelings of separation which makes it even more unworthy of love. Once the ego finds the courage to remove the mask it's wearing, it can stop repeating its dull unfulfilling life and step out of its darkness and into the light.

Removing the mask we are wearing allows us to start loving those unlovable parts in others, which they also believe are not lovable. Doing this, we gain the ability to love those unlovable aspects within ourselves. From this selfless place of loving and accepting whatever is inside others, we inadvertently heal ourselves. We find a selfless quality of love that feels truly powerful, courageous, and patient above all. There is a natural inclination to be kind with everyone and give as much as we can without feeling depleted. This path is real freedom, as it unmistakably brings out the best in everyone, making their hearts open to sing.

"And still, after all this time, the Sun has never said to the Earth, 'You owe me.'
Look what happens with love like that. It lights up the sky."
~ Rumi

When we meditate on what real love is, we discover that which is unchanging and never dies. We stop being attached to what is not real and find out what is real. We discover that the mind is not in charge, and the soul actually is. Through meditating on the source of real love, we transcend the perpetual swing of good and bad contradictions in the mind. The hypocritical thoughts cease to occur, and we awaken to a reality that has no criticisms about what we do or who we are.

Real love is that genuine movement of our soul in action. It is the most powerful healing energy in the Universe that can instantly transform everyone and everything. It instantly liberates any fearful, revengeful, or negative energy we may be caught in.

Real love turns every heavy personal issue that we're facing into one filled with a soft liberating lightness. The moment we open up our hearts to real love, we feel reborn, and a true magical alchemy takes place. Without this real love we are lost, and our busy lives feel like they are constantly falling apart as fast as we can put them together. With real love, we become the glue which holds everything together in its perfect place.

No matter whether we are battling with depression, anxiety, fear, or loneliness, this sweet soft healing force of real love is always there and alive inside of us. It arises in our heart naturally, with a simple patient request for it to come forth. By quietly asking real love to be more present in our lives, we will find that it spontaneously arises on its own accord. Love hears our thirsty call and beckons us to meet it at its deepest abyss.

By trusting in real love and making it our leading guide, we can relax about living this life. We are led to freedom each day, feeling the sweet surrender of our ego's grip that thinks life has to be a specific way. Life is not about getting all our personal needs met. There is something more important than obsessing about our own desires and fulfilling the desires of others. We are here to discover the deepest peace of our soul, find that unending state of gratitude and sacred appreciation for what is. With real love there is a sensation of always being guided towards this. We are innocently led on the perfect path to the highest destination and can feel that whatever we choose to do, we will be safe and provided for along the way.

At the core of your being you are *The Source of Love* itself. Your body is a natural loving machine which is designed to experience all the greatest pleasures in this world. It is a super sensitive vehicle that has magical qualities. When this body of magical love becomes the center of our lives, we start seeing the divinity that is all around us. We understand each moment holds the most perfect conditions and ingredients for our soul's highest awakening. There is no effort in making things happen in our lives; our highest manifestations naturally show up. We know we are all powerful beings who are fearlessly guided every single breath of the way. By realizing the source of love inside our hearts, we know that anything and everything is possible.

By allowing our hearts to be guided by gentleness, we discover the source of real love. The interactions we have with others become opportunities to evolve, heal, and rejuvenate ourselves. This love invokes us to live our greatest possible life and discover what it is our heart is truly after. When real love takes precedence over the ego, we stop hiding from life and start taking more risks to open up to others. We may allow ourselves to "fall in love" with someone and then later "rise in love" because we trust that the unconditional friendship of real love will always be there.

Real love is that missing sweet nutrient which allows our life purpose to sprout, blossom, and become fully self-realized. It's what makes your heart open, your mind, relax and the emotions deep enough so everything becomes crystal clear about why we are here on earth. Real love teaches us by example what we are supposed to do with our time here. By opening our heart to feeling the simple, soft, sweet, loving energy all around us each day, we will find a peace, compassion, and spiritual depth that satisfy our every human desire. With real love as our greatest guide, we naturally bring out the highest joy in others, which causes us to find even *more joy* within ourselves.

"This is love: to fly toward a secret sky, to cause a hundred veils to fall each moment.
First, to let go of life, and finally to take a step without feet."
~ Rumi

Real love is always here, shining behind it all. It is easily accessed inside you from a truly open and surrendered heart. It's always available, whenever we need it. When we rediscover that love is our essential nature, our heart is transformed into a vessel of forgiveness that assists all of humanity, touching the lives of everyone we meet. The greatest miracle of all occurs. People can no longer be with us and remain stuck in their darkness. They must transcend their contracted state and can no longer hurt themselves. Their heart, yearn to find this real love as well and becomes a conduit for the greater freedom. They find infinite compassion, eternal patience, and stop demanding that things be different than what they are. They instead move naturally closer towards their own heart, finding the real path of joy, appreciation, and zero resistance.

Simply through loving all the different parts of ourselves, we soon discover that we are the source of real love. We stop entertaining the movies of the neurotic mind and no longer identify with our victim stories. We find it more appealing to focus on that sacred spark within us which is truly divine. The most enlightening experience of our lives is found through loving what is. Loving what is includes loving every aspect of ourselves. This self-loving experience is not about being self-absorbed or selfish, yet simply honoring and recognizing the real divinity inside. We are seeing the greatest truth there is to see, as we open to the nakedness about who and what we really are.

I invite you to take this moment of your life right now to relax about the greatest issue you're currently facing. Imagine this issue is showing up on a movie screen in front of you, and the screen is getting smaller and smaller. The energy behind the issue is shrinking, becoming less and less real. The movie becomes so small that you can no longer see it, and you feel it disappearing from your life. Breathe in this feeling of relief into your body. Let yourself feel what it's like to let it go, and let yourself love yourself instead of this issue. Let love be your guide, and trust that it knows the way.

Are You Afraid of Being Rejected or Loved?

1. Do you feel unworthy or undeserving of love and attention? Why

2. Did you get attention/affection from your Mom and Dad?

3. Are you accustomed to being ignored by people? Example; Try to expand on these words to express how you may have felt about a past situation or person in your life:

I was made to feel I had no value and felt not worthwhile

No one listened to what I had to say…

I was ignored by my mom; by my dad

I was hit by my parents/guardian/care taker

I was yelled at, by my parents/guardian/caretaker

I was made to feel bad about myself

I was sexually abused by my caretaker/friend/brother/dad

I feel I am unlovable/that no will ever love me

How to Find the Love You Desire

Name

Date

Complete the lists below:

1. List the people to whom you can go to help you get a blind date or meet someone.

2. List the names of people who can introduce you to someone.

3. List the places in your city where you can go for fun, recreation or to meet a new date.

4. List four questions you would ask your new date and four activities or places you can go with your new date.

a.

b.

c.

A 7-Day Plan to Open Your Mind/Heart to Love

DAY 1
Self -Love

You must love yourself before anyone will love you. Meditate on this thought for today. Sit quietly and close your eyes for 10 minutes; then write any reflections or thoughts that come to mind.

If any thoughts come up during the day, write them on a sticky note and transfer them into your notebook before you go to bed at night.

DAY 2
Let Go All Fear

Let go all fear of the unknown.

Say, "I will breathe deeply and often throughout each day."

DAY 3
No One Can Hurts Me Without My Acceptance

Am I allowing someone to hurt me? When you practice knowing that YOU are enough, then the ego is not so easily snagged in its old game of never having enough. The ego's game is simply forcing you to go to the core of who you are and know that you are connected to the Spirit Source. When you stop and realize who you truly are, you instantly boost your vibration and feel empowered again. The ego is a desiring machine that is always wanting, wanting, wanting, and doesn't know what true satisfaction is. It is only through the heart that you can find this feeling of being enough. The day you can see that each experience in your life is a "spiritual experience" you will never have a problem again.

Negative thoughts naturally cannot rise in the mind, and you only have positive thoughts about yourself, the world, and everyone in it. Through living with the knowing that you are connected to everyone in this world, you begin overflowing with energy and love. Write or reflect on these words.

DAY 4
Give Up Your Need to Be Understood or Accepted

Write your understanding of this and what you will do to implement this.

Day 5
You Are Worthy to Be Loved

If no one has ever loved you in your life, become the first person who does. Write your understanding of this and what you will do to implement this.

Day 5
Love Affirmations

1. Love is who I am.

2. Love is eternal.

3. Love is everywhere.

4. I am love.

5. I am the love that I seek.

6. I am calling in my lover now.

7. I am love, I am love, I am love.

8. Love is all around me; I see it, I feel it, I speak it.

Day 6
Do You Have Issues With Abandonment?

Who abandoned or rejected you? Did not show love to you? At what age? Share your feelings

Will you allow this act, by someone who may have been self-centered or self-absorbed to determine yourself self-worth or self-value?

Write your understanding of this and what you will do to change this.

Day 7
How to Find the Love You Need

We all crave and need love. We are starving for love and feel deprived and lonely without it. I will let you in on the secret to fill your inner void for love. The Love You Seek Is Inside of You.

Start loving yourself to show others what kind of love you seek and desire.

Answer the questions below to help you identify what is missing in your love life:

What is your relationship like with men/women?

Imagine for a few moments that you can see, feel and experience your ideal partner. What would this person be like?

Can you imagine that you are best friends with him/her?

Write how you deal with your negative thoughts about men/women?

"No one is perfect... that is why pencils have erasers."
~ Author Unknown

"Lots of people want to ride with you in the limo,
but what you want is someone who will take the bus with
you when the limo breaks down."
~ Oprah Winfrey

The most I can do for my friend is simply be their friend.
~ Henry David Thoreau

Chapter 5

Follow Your Passion
to Find Love

The Universe and everything in it is perfect. One aspect of that perfection is that each of us has been given one or more talents/passions. When we express these talents, we are carrying out our role in the overall plan of the Universe. The Universe supports itself by encouraging each of us to fully and freely express our talents. If we want the support of the Universe, we must do what Spirit created us to do and that is to express our talents.

When we do that, we are encouraged by a feeling of comfort in our bodies. When we avoid doing that, we experience discomfort. In order for us to have a life that works perfectly, each of us must be doing in life what we were created to do and that is to express the talent or talents that are given to us to express. Our talents are gifts of the Universe. We do not learn a talent. Each talent we have been given is a gift that comes with the tools to express it perfectly. If we have artistic talent, we have all of the skills necessary to express that talent successfully.

We do not become better at a talent. We just gain confidence as we become more comfortable in expressing our talent more fully and freely. As we open ourselves, we surrender to the Universe and let "It" play through us. Expressing a talent is not a conscious mind experience. An artist or musician does not think about what colors or notes to select. When we let go of any sense of limitation, we become totally intuitive and allow the infinite supply of energy to flow freely through us. It is an experience of freedom and joy, not thought and effort.

When we release all limitations, extraordinary things happen. When we are expressing our talents and passions fully and freely, we experience perfection. If only we could take a pill that would release all of our negative thoughts and open us to the Universe and its infinite supply of energy, we would express ourselves with total magnificence. Then and only then will we experience the joy and bliss of following our passion. When we follow our passion we are more alive, more vibrant, we have a love sparkle that can catch the attention of the love partner who is right for us. And who is just waiting to connect their love with our passion which could be the same as their passion.

Jealousy is Not Love
Love is not jealousy.
Love is not need.
Love is not ownership.
Love is not hoarding.
Love is not clinging.
Love is not restricting.
Love is not prohibiting.
Love is not bondage.
Love is not slavery.
Love is not dependency.
Love is not possession.
Jealousy is not love.
Imagine a world without jealousy.

Love is a revolving door. It is the many chambers of yourself and your life. The heart is an open chamber that is always looking for ways to help you evolve spiritually, and we do this evolution through the mechanism of love. Love truly is a many splendored thing; It is exciting, it is thrilling, and love is captivating.

These are some steps you can take to empower yourself as you reframe your relationship strategies, beliefs, and outcomes.

1. Realize that it is not okay for your needs and desires to be ignored. Notice if this is what has happened in the past, and make a goal to correct the situation. Because you can find true love if that is what you truly want.

2. Recognize the recurring themes in your love life to get you back on the path to find true love.

3. Change your beliefs about yourself and your relationship habits.

4. Develop self-awareness. Know who you are and be your authentic loving self.

5. Stop being too busy focusing on other people, and make more time to focus on yourself and your love needs.

6. Sit down with yourself and outline what is important to you. Identify the core values of your life for your family, health, career, and relationships. This will determine the decisions you make about who or what you want your love life to be or look like.

Identify any limiting beliefs you have about yourself in relation to love and decide not to accept them anymore. If you believe you have to be the caretaker and to never nurtured in return, know that about yourself so you can release that belief and find a life partner who aligns with your new belief that you are worthy of attention and love. Write your values down in order of importance. Doing this will help you understand your priorities and recognize a partner who shares those key values.

7. Identify your needs for what you want in a relationship. It is okay to have needs, it is normal, and vital that they be recognized and acknowledged in order for you to be happy in love. Notice your needs for affection, openness, communication, consideration, commitment, and trust.

8. Know your relationship requirements and settle for nothing less. Perhaps you fooled yourself into thinking there is a limited number of possible partners, and that you have to take what you can get or be alone. Unfortunately, that kind of thinking is a limiting belief and a self-fulfilling prophecy. When you expect less, you get less.

9. Define what you want; figure that out and persevere. Trust that if you apply yourself you can get what you really want in your life.

Remember, you must be able to say NO to what you DON'T want, to be able to say YES to what you DO want.

LOVE	FEAR
Coming from Love	**Coming from Fear**
Responsibility	Victim
Pro-Active	Re-Active
Towards	Away From
Own Shadows	Defensive, Denial
Growth Experience in Life	Resist Change/Stay in Comfort Zone
Open/Vulnerable	Protected/Attacking
Ask for Help	Do it Myself
Joy/Bliss/Curiosity/Peaceful	Anger/Sadness/Competition
Live in the Moment	Fear Future/Hold Onto
Empower/Mentor	Control/Dominate
Be of Service, Hear	Use Fix
Pain as Sensation, Information	Pain as Suffering, Bad
Learn Lesson	Withdraw/Punish
Connection	Isolation
Observations/Evaluations/Choice Does it Work or Not? Is it Empowering? I Could	Judgment/Control Is it Good or Bad? Is it Right or Wrong? I Should
Vision/Mission	Survival
Seek to Understand/Compassion	Judge/Blame
Go Through Fear (Conscious Choice)	Fight/Flight (Unconscious Choice)
Grateful	Jealous/Envious/Needy
Intention/Surrender	Expectation/Attachment
Ask for What I Want	Manipulate

When you live your life aligned with your core values you will feel on track and fulfill one of your highest needs: for your life to have meaning. Be your authentic self. If you are able to identify our core values and limiting beliefs, you've taken the first step towards being your authentic self. Embrace your core values and overcome your limiting beliefs and voila! You will find that you are attracting like-minded people and automatically deterring those who do not belong in your life. You will have created space for the right person to show up.

Knowing what makes you "**you**" will help you recognize when you are acting to maintain a relationship in a way that goes against your grain. That self-knowledge will warn you when you act in opposition of your core values. It will also alert you when you are reacting according to limiting beliefs. When you notice either of these things happening, stop and remind yourself of your end goal: a committed long term relationship that supports, enriches, and warms you, and act accordingly.

Think of a time when one of your needs was not met in a relationship. Did you feel hurt, angry, frustrated, unappreciated, or something similar? Being aware of your needs and that they are legitimate will help you to know when they are not being met. Awareness will help you quickly recognize when and if you are slipping into your old familiar pattern of not caring for your own needs first. Changing the automatic response patterns you've developed over the years requires mental intervention and physical action.

You have the power to choose who, what, where, when, and how, and get the relationship you really want. Develop a dating strategy and act upon it. Set your dating GPS to get to the relationship you deserve, and then follow the steps until you arrive safely. When you catch yourself getting off course and falling into your old familiar patterns, stop and re-evaluate your dating or relationship plans for your life. When you go against the innate response of your learned pattern it will feel uncomfortable or unnatural, because it's been well practiced and is all too familiar.

With the help of a Relationship Coach you can break your old destructive habits of looking for love in all the wrong places. To have lasting love you must look inside yourself to become a whole person. No one wants to connect or be in relationship with an emotionally handicapped or incomplete person. Complete yourself, and you will be attractive to another complete person. It is critical that you know how you present yourself to others and to the world.

Do you present yourself as a weak, helpless person who needs someone to take care of her/him or do you show others your strengths? It is unfair to you and the other person if you present yourself as weak to attract someone and then let your strong self, show up after you are in a relationship. Do not highjack your character or integrity just to be in a relationship with someone. If you are true to your inner self, you will one day attract a man who is deserving of you.

Do not let yourself be pressured by time or things people may say to you. Some people are supposed to be in a relationship and some are not. Look inside yourself to see what is your life's, purpose and why you are here on the planet. I was not supposed to have children so that I could be a foster mom, an adopted mom, and to counsel the many children I now counseled.

Chapter 6

How to Find the Love
You Want

According to Fenny Smedley, life therapist, angel intuitive, author of 20 books, and award-winning lyricist, most people automatically think in terms of a partner, chemistry, a life-long union, so they are often disappointed because this is not always the case. Also many people believe that there is only one soul mate for them in the entire world. This is inaccurate too. It's possible to have many different soul mates of different kinds. What kinds of soul mates are there? There are opinions on how many kinds of soul mates there are, everywhere you look, but my experience has made me believe in four main kinds:

Eternal Flames: This is what most people picture when they think of perfect soul mates. This is someone who feels like half of you. Whenever they're absent, your life almost seems to go on hold. They know what you are thinking and they offer you total unconditional love. There will be no battlefields with them; only maybe minor skirmishes as both parties have to learn their own lessons, but the partnership embodies the saying that together, two people are greater than the sum of their parts. There will be no unfaithfulness, because the love these people feel goes down to a soul level, and it will be impossible for them to hurt each other, and they will never desire any other person. Not everyone will find this kind of soul mate in every life they live. Because of the strong dependency that can be formed, this is not always a good thing, and it might not be right at this particular stage of their existence.

Because of this we may live some lifetimes apart from our Eternal Flame, just to make sure that we learn to rely on ourselves and not on someone else.

Twin Soul Mates: One step down, in a way, from Eternal Flames, this can be the most confusing type of soul mate of all, because love is certainly and obviously there between them. They can be very alike in many ways, and they seem familiar right from their first meeting—and they are familiar, because you will always have known them before, in other lifetimes. They make you feel comfortable, because in a past life they were probably your friend or partner, and it's tempting to think you can just take up where you left off with them. It is an instinctual pull, and sometimes it is right. But this is where the trouble can come, because often they are just there to help you out, and often not meant to be your lifelong partner. Not realizing this, and perhaps being pressured to commit by social peers, you might marry this twin soul and then further down the line find you need to part. Or you can be meant to be partners for a short time, perhaps to create specific children, and once those children have been created the need to be together disappears.

Teacher Soul Mates: There is a saying: "When the pupil is ready, the teacher will appear." Soul mates of this kind will sometimes come into our lives, usually temporarily, to enable us to learn something vital to our soul's progress. They will not normally be a partner, but this can happen. The relationship can be challenging and difficult. And the lesson can be harsh. However, once the lesson has been given, this person will sometimes vanish as mysteriously as they appeared, and this can cause us to feel upset and confused.

Comforter Soul Mates: They can step into your life, sometimes to just say a specific word, or do a certain thing, or bring comfort and companionship when you're feeling alone, or offer some advice to help you make a tricky decision. They are often lifelong friends once they appear. They think the same way as you and are always there for you, but you never see them as a potential partner. They are often the opposite sex, and yet there is no sexual chemistry between the two of you. This is a true platonic relationship.

Love is Something You Do; It Is Action

Love is not a noun. It involves your taking some action if you want to find love or be in a loving relationship. Listed below are some actions you will need to take to increase your chances of finding the love you want. They are: Respect, Accountability, Accommodation, Reciprocity, Compromise, and Mutuality.

Respect: Showing the type of respect in my words and actions that reflects how I wish to be respected and in turn, shows how I respect myself (i.e., setting personal boundaries in a healthy, assertive manner).

Accountability: Taking responsibility for my own verbal and nonverbal behaviors in the relationship, particularly those verbal and non-verbal behaviors that are hurtful to another person, or do I use some form of self-protection that deflects responsibility for my behaviors to some other source (i.e., become contemptuous, become defensive, become critical, or stonewall).

Accommodation: Making room/space for a partner or giving of myself for a partner (i.e., living together, becoming an inter-dependent couple, both the "we" and the individual "me" as part of the sharing in a partner's interest if the partner desires this).

Reciprocity: It is giving behaviors in a relationship. You want to be careful to avoid keeping score or expecting something in return. If you want ease in your relationship, give for the sake of giving because it gives you joy to please your partner.

Compromise: Being able to reach an agreement that is acceptable to both partners whether this agreement involves choosing to support/accept one partner's wishes, or finding the middle ground, or agreeing to disagree.

Mutuality: Working as a team to solve a problem, creating mutually agreed on goals for the future, and finding commonalities that defines you as a couple rather than individuals in a relationship.

The Five Languages of Love

Here are the five primary ways we give and receive love according to author Gary Chapman:

• Words of affirmation
• Quality time
• Gifts
• Acts of service
• Physical touch

The Many Faces of Love

We tend to forget that life, no matter what aspect of living we may be focused on, is about our evolution. Our earthling mind may forget this great truth, but our "Soul" would never let such important information be overlooked—not even for a minute. It is because your SOUL has come directly from Source/Spirit/The Creator, and absolutely understands this, for it is a cornerstone of creation. Therefore, your Soul would also understand that the *reason* for having a "Soul Lover" or a "Soul Mate" is for your shared evolution, and the express purpose is so that the two of you can facilitate each other's growth.

But there is much more to a soul connection than that, and that's where Spirit comes in to guide you to the right person. Spirit teaches you not only how to recognize and harvest the wonderful growth that you and your Soul Mate(s) will be generating for each other, but also how to love that growth and still love each other. It also teaches how to keep expanding that growth, use that growth to achieve your destiny, and have fun together doing it or not doing it. Some soul lessons may not be fun, but are necessary for your soul's evolution.

This is only possible when you live your "Soul's Intelligence", when you are open to receive inner guidance from your High Self or Divine Self. When you receive the "Inner Guidance" to understand, you surrender your will to the Divine and open your heart to be open to receive lover. When you allow this illumined understanding to empower your growth, then your spiritual growth will allow you to step all the way into your life's destiny.

You Deserve Love

Ultimately love is self-approval.

Love is the place you are coming from, your ground of being. You are love.

Love is the divine force everywhere, the universal energy, the moving power of life that flows in your own heart.

Love is accepting someone as he or she is and as he or she is not.

Love is the acknowledgement of a union that already exists.

You already are part of this universal unifying essence called love. In addition, you are either loving or not loving. If you are a loving person, people will feel your attractive force and will appear in your path so you can love them. And there are multitudes of people who want to express their love to you. It is important to realize however, that you cannot accept any more love than you are willing to give yourself. Many people have had so much disapproval in life that they have forgotten how to go about loving themselves.

What is Self-Love?

Self-love is acknowledging & praising yourself out loud to yourself.
Self-love is approving of all your actions.
Self-love is having confidence in your ability.
Self-love is giving yourself pleasures without guilt.
Self-love is loving your body and admiring your beauty.
Self-love is giving yourself what you want and feeling you deserve it.
Self-love is letting yourself win.
Self-love is letting others in instead of submitting to loneliness.
Self-love is following your own intuition.
Self-love is making your own rules responsibly.
Self-love is seeing your own perfection.
Self-love is taking credit for what you did.
Self-love is surrounding yourself with beauty,
Self-love is letting yourself be rich and not staying in poverty.
Self-love is creating an abundance of friends.
Self-love is rewarding yourself, never punishing yourself.
Self-love is trusting yourself.
Self-love is nourishing yourself with good food and good ideas.
Self-love is surrounding yourself with people who nourish you.
Self-love is enjoying sex.
Self-love is getting a massage frequently.

Self-love is seeing yourself as equal to others.
Self-love is forgiving yourself and others.
Self-love is letting in affection.
Self-love is authority over yourself, not giving it away to another.
Self-love is developing your creative drives.
Self-love is having fun all the time.
Self-love is really talking to yourself gently and lovingly.
Self-love is becoming your own approving inner parent.
Self-love is turning all your negative thoughts into affirmations.

If you have a good relationship with yourself, you will automatically have a good relationship with others. "The soul attracts that which is secretly harbors." In other words, you will attract the person who has harmony with your thought structures. If you feel really good about yourself, you'll attract someone who feels good about him/herself. By the universal law of attraction, someone will respond to the mental vibrations you exude.

You can create the perfect relationship for yourself by sitting down and listing the things you want in such a relationship. Meditate on them. Imagine already having such a relationship. Imagine the person you want for a partner. If you really are willing for it to happen, someone will come into your life just as you imagine, by this universal law of attraction. Thought creates vibrations which inevitably attract that which is in its image.

If you are already in a relationship, the same procedure will work. Picture these positive, divine qualities coming out in him/her. Your partner will soon develop and become as you imagine. Jesus often spoke of the law of attraction. "As you believe, so shall it be done unto you." "Unto him who hath, shall be given." When you come to understand that there is only one universal mind which is every place at the same time and in all things, you will see that the differences between you are others are illusionary. We are all the same; we are just vibrating at different levels of energy. When you raise your energy vibration level, you will attract people on higher and higher energy levels.

Do not dwell on thoughts of the lack of things. There are no limitations. There is no lack in the universal mind of Spirit in which we are all a part. Whatever you ask for you will be given. However, you must believe and expect that what you want will happen. So watch yourself and watch your thoughts. If you are thinking, "I'll never meet somebody who _____ ", you never will. Immediately invert the thought to something like this:

"I am now attracting someone who _____ ".

What you are willing to accept will come your way. Ken Keyes said, "Happiness is experienced when life gives you what you are willing to accept." So take responsibility for the thoughts you choose to think regarding your relationships. You can bring people you like into your life with your thoughts. The logical person to put in your circle is someone with whom you are in harmony or whomever you think you deserve.

Let's say you are now in a caring, fulfilling, loving relationship. You may wonder how to make or keep it successful. It's easy. A successful relationship is based upon one person being nourished by the other person's presence. If you just do that, it's enough. You don't have to do anything else except set up certain agreements you will both keep. You can make it a game, but don't get stuck in the rules of how you think the other should be or act. You might want to change your rules of how to be in a relationship as frequently as every week. Learn to negotiate what you want, need, or choose to have.

Are You Looking to Find Love As a Mother/Wife?

I am still looking at how I can get adults to move into a natural play mode rather in some of the artificial ways that some adults use like alcohol and recreational drugs, which tend to cloud their spirit of play. Children are into natural play, so I do not have to coach them on how to play. They have problems when they are trying to be who they are and learn how to live with a parent who is into an artificial place. It is easy for me to counsel a child on how to live with a crazy parent. For the mom it will take some counseling for her to let go of her artificial form of play (drugs) and later coach her on how to go back to her natural playful child that she has lost. My challenge is how I can get the insurance company to pay for my counseling of her and her child. She has money issues and is now looking for how she can set aside her money to provide for her son in the future. I realize now I that I can get paid to help people solve problems, I want to figure out how to get people to pay me to coach them on how to play or help them re-learn how to play.

These are some insights Christian Carter shares about men and about why men withdraw from a relationship. He says once women understand it will stop a lot of the pain and frustration women experience with dating and relationships. When a man gets truly close to a woman and deeply intimate, for any extended period of time, he loves that feeling and wants more of it. But the strange part of this is that the moment a man experiences this period of intense closeness, he will take some space for himself.

I know this sounds counter-intuitive, but it is how most men work emotionally. Most men will actually seek some amount of space to "recover". It's kind of like how after a muscle gets worked out it needs to rest before it can grow stronger and be active again. Men can become distant even in good relationships, and if you know what to do, you can keep a guy physically and emotionally engaged even when he needs time to recover.

And there's another reason why a man might withdraw that has nothing whatsoever to do with the women; he's not living his "purpose".

The Importance of Purpose For a Man

It's important for a man to be clear about what he's doing in his own life and what his purpose is. A man's purpose can be anything from something straightforward like excelling at work or building his own company, to something more creative like starting and working at a do-it-yourself project at home or training at his favorite sport.

The point is that a man has some goals and is engaged and focused on doing something and doing it well. A man's purpose is essential to his overall emotional and social well-being. But often times, even men themselves aren't clear on what their purpose is, or don't really go after their purpose and assert themselves.

How a Man's Purpose (or Lack of) Can Affect a Woman

When a man isn't going after his own purpose, or has fallen away from it, or forgotten about it, it often gets in the way of the relationship he's in. Men become withdrawn, restless, irritated, and seem generally unengaged in life as a whole. They stop initiating plans. They stop spending as much time with people, even their own friends. They shut the world out. And of course, they become emotionally withdrawn and distant as well.

Too often men aren't conscious that this is what's happening to them, and they end up pulling away from their relationship and making things even worse for themselves. This is when they often seem to go in and out of being present and engaged in the relationship and then completely withdrawn.

They slide between the two largely because of the way that they're feeling about themselves or how things are going for them in the world as it relates to their purpose. And often women take on the problems the man is going through and try to help, or even mistake his behavior to mean something about his feelings, about them or the relationship. So, now that we know that a man's withdrawing is not automatically the woman's fault, she can nothing do about it.

What Doesn't Work In Love for Men

There are certain behaviors and approaches women often take when their man starts withdrawing, and they usually work against the woman. Let's get those out of the way so we know what NOT to do...

Approach #1: Convincing Him

If you're a woman, when you're with a man who is feeling or acting uncertain with you, trying to convince him otherwise puts you in a very dangerous and weak position for your relationship, even if you give him an ultimatum that would move things ahead to the place in your relationship that you want. Why? Because he's not really making that decision based on what he wants or feels.

What you really want and need is a man who is truly committed to being with you on a physical, mental, emotional, and even spiritual level. Not coerced, not forced, not convinced.

Approach #2: Over Sharing Your Feelings

If you're like most women, then you think sharing your feelings with a man first, and often, will somehow get him to share his feelings in return. But this isn't how it works for a man. You can share your feelings with a man, but to expect that this will encourage him to do the same with you will only lead you to unnecessary frustration, especially if a man is already acting withdrawn. When a man acts withdrawn, that's a signal that he is undergoing his own emotional process and needs time to recharge. Once he's ready to share his feelings, he'll be back. But trying to stimulate him to do so, by becoming overly emotional won't work.

Approach #3: Setting Unrealistic Expectations

Women tend to think that if things are going well with a guy, that he will naturally want to move things forward to the next level. They'll just assume this even when the guy has never talked about the future. So you know what happens next. Things will be coasting along, and suddenly the guy will change gears, she'll find out he's dating other women, or he doesn't make plans with her every weekend, and she's left wondering what the heck happened.

The answer is that the woman created all these expectations about what the relationship was supposed to look like and how he was supposed to behave, and when he fell short of that, she became disappointed and unfulfilled. This usually winds up in a confrontation that causes tension and maybe even creates more distance. The flip side of this is that a woman will try to pretend she's okay with just a casual relationship, gets closer to him thinking he'll "come around", and then becomes disappointed when he doesn't.

Approach #4: Having "The Talk"

As an independent thinking woman who is used to getting out there and getting what she wants in her career and the rest of her life, it might seem like laying your cards on the table and having a talk with a man about "where the relationship is going" is the sensible, adult way to move things forward. You might think that if you give him all your reasons for why you two are perfect for each other, like you'd do in a job interview, it will make him open his eyes and realize he'd be a fool to have things any other way. But think about this: Do men truly commit and choose to love and become loyal, caring, affectionate, etc. just because a woman asks them?

No. A man needs to have his own reasons for being and feeling this way, and this happens when he feels a deep emotional attraction for you.

Affirmations to Improve or Change Your Relationships

I, _____ (your name) now approve of
_____ (other person's name) and take responsibility for my feelings of jealousy.

The more freedom I give my partner the more he/ she loves me.
I no longer need _____ (other person's name) for my survival so it does not matter if he/she has other behavior patterns.

I, _____ no longer need to see
_____ as my father/mother and struggle to get his/her love.

I, _____ am now willing to let my incestuous feelings toward my father/mother surface.

I _____ now take responsibility to establish agreements about outside relationships.

I _____ am careful not to use outside relationships as a form of manipulation.

I_____ no longer need to set _____ up as my mother or father.

I_____ no longer expect _____to show love to me in this manner.

I now let _____communicate openly in a harmonious way.

I no longer need the dramatic outbursts I used as a child to get attention, now that I love and accept myself.

Since you have no guarantee that your partner will be faithful, it is better to work on the affirmation "I _____ now approve of _____ and take responsibility for my feelings of jealousy" so I can better handle any feelings of jealousy and take the pressure off my companion.

When your partner notices "your" approving attitude or behavior, he/she will appreciate it. He/she may be confused at first, because it may be hard for them to believe they are getting the approval they wanted. The game playing will be over because the old payoff will longer be there. Just getting in touch with your underlying purposes in the game playing will help both of you to change. It can be very releasing when you take a more mature approach to your relationship building skills and give yourself an option for outside relationship building, even if it is on a limited basis.

How to Grow Love Inside to Be In a Relationship

We create what we most desire and what we most fear. Often times we get watered down results because part of us wants something, but another part of us is afraid to get it. This is called "approach avoidance". Sometimes this happens in the game of finding and creating a love relationship. This is a fear of going for what you want; like wanting to date an attractive partner but being afraid to strike up a conversation. All fears are fears of feelings our emotions either emotional feelings or physical feelings. Everything that we are afraid that might happen is really a fear of how we would feel if it were to happen. We manifest situations that make us feel uncomfortable or that we are afraid of so we can reintegrate emotions that we've been avoiding since we were little and we felt overwhelmed by intense emotional feelings. All fears are resolvable.

In the game of love you do not need hide or seek, you are always found by love. Love is inside of you. Love may manifest as friendship, romance, service or a warm feeling. The innate, infinite love of Divine Source is with you always. You are never separate from it. It loves you beyond measure. When you accept this love for yourself as real and incorporate it inside of you, you will begin to feel more love for yourself and more loving. Daily acknowledge and accept this love within you for 30 to 60 days.

Soon you will begin to feel more loving and then you can give the love you feel inside you away to another person. Continue this practice over and over until you feel genuine love inside you. Don't let your intellect get involved. Love is a feeling, you cannot think about love. You have to develop and become the love you want to receive from another person. For it is only then that you will have enough love to give to another person. Start today, to grow the love inside you until you feel a fullness; when you feel genuine love inside of you, you will have love to give to another from your overflow. *No one can give you love, you cannot buy love; you cannot eat love, you cannot find love,* **you can only be love. Be the Love You Want to Have or Receive.**

Until you feel love inside of you; you are not ready to be in a relationship with another person, nor will you be capable to be in a love relationship with another person. You cannot give water from an empty bucket; likewise you cannot give love to another person if you are empty of love inside you. All relationships require you to be intimate with the other person. Intimacy is a close, familiar and affectionate, loving, personal relationship with another person. It is where you share your private thoughts, feelings, wants, needs, fears, secrets, fantasies, and desires; you share everything inside you without holding anything back.

A loving relationship requires you to have commitment to yourself, the other person and to the relationship. Commitment creates safety for yourself, and safety for your partner. You continually take risks and allow yourself to be vulnerable. Tell the whole truth; then expect and ask for a positive response from your partner You can learn how to release your fears so that you can take action and manifest what you want in your relationship by using the 'Emotional Reintegration" technique.

Emotional Reintegration is a process where instead of avoiding uncomfortable feelings, you embrace and reintegrate them into your body. You do this by being fully present to the feelings that are coming up for you, notice where in your body the feeling is the strongest. Be unconditionally accepting of the feeling until it moves, shifts, expands, and ultimately dissipates from your body. This can take a few seconds, a few minutes, or a few hours. Remember to stay focused on the physical sensations without analyzing it, judging it, or trying to make it go away. If you would like assistance or coaching with this technique, I can be contacted by E-mail: ida@thejourneytoselflove.com

How to Create and Sustain a Healthy Relationship

We each have our own model of the world. Everybody wants something. To gain a deeper level of rapport enter the other person's world, and view their experience from their perspective.

One of the keys to connecting is to enter the other person's world. The second key to connecting with another person is to listen with the intention to hear and learn and the third gem is to be fully present in the moment. Forget about your agenda and focus on connecting with the person in front of you. Focus on this person and really listen to what they have to say about themselves, their life and the situations they are confronting.

If you are dating or starting a new relationship it is to best to make a reasonable request at a reasonable time ex. Can I call you in a week or a few days if it is business? If this is a romantic relationship, find out what the other person likes to do and I suggest you make plans to do that with them on your next date or meeting. When you are on a date, focus your attention on the person in front of you.

Remember, who you are is Spirit's gift to you, and what you make of yourself with the use of your gifts, talents and time on the planet is your gift to the Divine. Develop your gifts and talents so that you make a difference on the planet. Daily Let Your Best Self show up. Because, you bought this book, you are entitled to a complimentary 30-minute Strategy session with me to help you look at ways to revive a relationship, create a new relationship or create a plan of action on how to find the love of your life. Go to www.journeytoselflove.com to get your Complimentary Strategy session. Email: ida@thejourneytoselflove.com

About the Author

Dr. Ida Greene shares her magical strategies with people through Speaking, Journey to Self-Love Coaching Workshops, Webinar, Tele-Summits, Trainings, and Retreats. Dr. Ida is available as an Inspirational Keynote Speaker, and Motivational Speaker. The goal is to help you move through the barriers that keep you from being your best in your personal and professional life.

She is a highly gifted Intuitive Healer, providing: Clairaudient Messages, Past Life Regressions, Energy Clearing, Angel Readings, and Reiki Energy balancing sessions by phone appointments, 619-262-9951.

Dr. Greene coaches on "How to Be Alone, Without Feeling Lonely", "Looking for Love, In All the Wrong Places" and helps you Master Your Personal Power on Your Journey to Self-Love, through her Journey to Self-Love Coaching, Workshops and Retreats.

To get your Complimentary Self Love Strategy Session go to: **www.journeytoselflove.com** E-mail: ida@thejourneytoselflove.com
www.idagreene.com, www.greatnesstravel.com
Our books are available at **www.idagreeene.com**, Amazon, and Barnes and Noble.

Journey To Self-Love Coaching, Workshops and Retreats

Dr. Ida Greene shares her magical strategies with people through Speaking, Journey to Self-Love Coaching Workshops, Webinar, Tele-Summits, Trainings, and Retreats. Dr. Ida is available as an Inspirational Keynote Speaker, and Motivational Speaker. The goal is to help you move through the barriers that keep you from being your best in your personal and professional life.

Dr. Ida Greene, PhD

www.ingramcontent.com/pod-product-compliance
Lightning Source LLC
Chambersburg PA
CBHW052135090426
42741CB00009B/2084